For Liz Sohappy Bahe

For Jim Barnes

This book is the fifth in Harper & Row's Native American Publishing Program. All profits from this program are set aside in a special fund and used to support projects designed to aid the Native American people.

Other books in the program

Seven Arrows, by Hyemeyohsts Storm

Ascending Red Cedar Moon, by Duane Niatum

Winter in the Blood, by James Welch

Indians' Summer, by Nasnaga

CARRIERS OF THE DREAM WHEEL

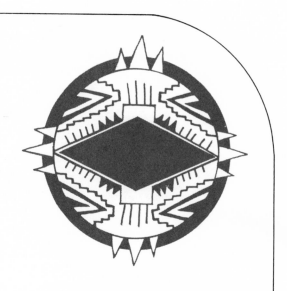

CARRIERS
OF THE
DREAM WHEEL

Contemporary Native American Poetry
Edited by Duane Niatum

Harper & Row, Publishers
New York   Evanston   San Francisco   London

To our people

Because this page cannot accommodate all acknowledg-
ments, they appear on the following three pages.

Library of Congress Cataloging in Publication Data

Niatum, Duane, 1938–   comp. Carriers of the Dream Wheel.
contents: Liz Sohappy Bahe.—Jim Barnes.—Joseph
Bruchac. [etc.] 1. American poetry—Indian authors.
2. American poetry—20th century.   I. Title.
PS591.I55N5 1975   811'.5'408   74–5986
ISBN 0–06–451151–0

FIRST EDITION

Book design by Susan Mitchell
Drawings by Wendy Rose

Acknowledgments

Some of the poems in this book have previously appeared in the following publications to which the authors and publisher gratefully acknowledge permission to reprint:

AFTER THE DEATH OF AN ELDER KLALLAM by Duane Niatum: *Old Woman Awaiting the Greyhound Bus; On Visiting My Son, Port Angeles, Washington; The Novelty Shop; After the Death of an Elder Klallam; On Hearing the Marsh Bird's Water Cry* and *Elegy for Chief Sealth (1786–1866).* Permission granted by Baleen Press, P.O. Box 13448, Phoenix, AZ, publisher of *After the Death of an Elder Klallam,* © 1970 by Duane McGinnis.

AMERICAN POETRY REVIEW, vol. 2, no. 6: *Stone Giant* by Joseph Bruchac; *A Nation Wrapped in Stone; Direction; Dream of Rebirth; Lines for Marking Time* and *Beginning the Year at Rosebud, S.D.* by Roberta Hill; *Please Forward; Across the Peloponnese; Why I Didn't Go to Delphi* and *Verifying the Dead* by James Welch; *In Dream: The Privacy of Sequence* and *Waiting to Be Fed* by Ray A. Young Bear.

ASCENDING RED CEDAR MOON by Duane Niatum: *Ascending Red Cedar Moon; Chief Leschi of the Nisqually; Homage to Chagall; On Leaving Baltimore; No One Remembers Abandoning the Village of White Fir; Indian Rock, Bainbridge Island, Washington; Slow Dancer That No One Hears but You* and *To Your Question.* Harper & Row, © 1974 by Duane Niatum.

FROM THE BELLY OF THE SHARK, Walter Lowenfels, ed.: *Dragon Skate* by Gladys Cardiff; *Oh My People I Remember* by Wendy Rose. Random House/Vintage Books, 1973.

THE BUFFALO IN THE SYRACUSE ZOO by Joseph Bruchac: *For a Winnebago Brave.* © 1972, Greenfield Review Press.

CHICAGO REVIEW: *Indian Song: Survival* and *Prayer to the Pacific* by Leslie Silko, © 1973, Chicago Review, vol. 24, no. 4; *Crow's Way* by Duane Niatum, © 1974, Chicago Review, vol. 25, no. 1.

COME TO POWER, Dick Lourie, ed.: *These Horses Came* and *Another Face* by Ray A. Young Bear. Crossing Press, 1974.

CONCERNING POETRY: *Halcyon Days* by Jim Barnes, vol. 6, no. 1, Spring 1973, reprinted by permission; *Arizona Highways* by James Welch, vol. 4, no. 1, Spring 1971, reprinted by permission.

DACOTAH TERRITORY, no. 6, Winter 1973–74, James L. White, guest ed.: *In the Madison Zoo* and *Whispers* by Roberta Hill; *The Creation: According to Coyote* by Simon Ortiz; *Manifest Destiny; Eclipse* and *In the Flight of the Blue Heron: To Montezuma* by Anita Endrezze Probst.

EDGE: *Critter* and *Message from Ohanapecosh Glacier* by W. M. Ransom.

FINDING TRUE NORTH by W. M. Ransom: *Critter, Grandpa's .45; Indian Summer: Montana, 1956; On the Morning of the Third Night Above Nisqually* and *Catechism, 1958.* © 1973, Copper Canyon Press.

GRANITE: *Hiking* by Joseph Bruchac

GREENFIELD REVIEW: *To Insure Survival* by Simon Ortiz. Greenfield Review Press.

HOPI ROADRUNNER DANCING by Wendy Rose: *For My People; Oh Father; Self-Dirge; Epitaph; Grunion* and *Oh My People I Remember.* © 1973, Greenfield Review Press.

INDIAN MOUNTAIN AND OTHER POEMS by Joseph Bruchac: *IV; Three Poems for the Indian Steelworkers in a Bar Where I Used to Drink; Coming Back; Poem for Jan; City; Second Skins—A Peyote Song* and *Frozen Hands.* © 1971, Ithaca House.

INDIAN VOICE: *Manifest Destiny* and *Eclipse* by Anita Endrezze Probst.

INSCAPE: *Grey Woman* by Gladys Cardiff. Reprinted from *Inscape*, vol. , 1, no. 3, new series, by permission of Baleen Press, P.O. Box 13448, Phoenix, AZ.

INTRO #1, R. V. Cassill, ed.: *Song for Healing* by Roberta Hill. © 1968 by Bantam Books Inc. Reprinted by permission.

INVISIBLE CITY: *Frozen Hands* by Joseph Bruchac.

IRONWOOD, 1973: *Catechism, 1958* by W. M. Ransom

KEEPER OF ARROWS, POEMS FOR THE CHEYENNE by Lance Henson: *The Cold; Grandfather; Moon at Three* A.M.; *Our Smoke Has Gone Four Ways; Dawn in January; Last Words, 1968* and *Wish.* Renaissance Press, 1972.

LAGUNA WOMAN by Leslie Silko: *Toe-osh: A Laguna Coyote Story* and *Poem for Ben Barney.* Greenfield Review Press, 1974.

MALAHAT REVIEW, May 1973: *Exodus; The Stripper* and *The Truth About My Sister and Me* by Anita Endrezze Probst. University of Victoria (British Columbia).

MISSISSIPPI REVIEW, 1974: *Sweating It Out on Winding Stair Mountain* by Jim Barnes.

MISSOURI POET: *Camping Out on Rainy Mountain* by Jim Barnes.

NEW AMERICAN REVIEW #14: *Directions to the Nomad* by James Welch.

NEW COLLAGE, 1974: *Lying in a Yuma Saloon* by Jim Barnes.

NEW YORK QUARTERLY: *Farewell* by Liz Sohappy Bahe.

NORTHWEST REVIEW, vol. 13, no. 2: *Last Look at La Plata, Missouri* by Jim Barnes; *To Frighten a Storm* and *Long Person* by Gladys Cardiff; *Falling Moon* by Roberta Hill; *The Way the Bird Sat* by Ray A. Young Bear.

PANACHE, 1974: *Autobiography: Last Chapter* by Jim Barnes.

PEMBROKE MAGAZINE: *Poem for Diane Wakoski* and *Rushing* by Ray A. Young Bear.

PHOENIX: *War Walking Near* by Ray A. Young Bear.

POETRY NORTHWEST, vol. 13, no. 4: *Star Quilt* and *Sleeping with Foxes* by Roberta Hill. © 1973, Poetry Northwest.

PRAIRIE SCHOONER: *These Damned Trees Crouch* by Jim Barnes; *Old Woman Awaiting a Greyhound Bus* by Duane Niatum. © 1970 by the University of Nebraska Press. Reprinted by permission from *Prairie Schooner*.

PUGET SOUNDINGS, March 1971: *Combing* by Gladys Cardiff. Reprinted by permission of the Junior League of Seattle.

RIDING THE EARTHBOY 40 by James Welch: *Surviving; D–Y Bar; The Renegade Wants Words; In My Lifetime; Magic Fox; Blue Like Death; Snow Country Weavers; The Man from Washington; Going to Remake This World; Harlem, Montana: Just Off the Reservation; In My First Hard Springtime* and *Christmas Comes to Moccasin Flat.* World Publishing Co., 1971.

ST. ANDREWS REVIEW, vol. 2, no. 2 (1973): *The Captive Stone* by Jim Barnes.

SALT LICK: *City* by Joseph Bruchac.

SENECA REVIEW: *The Crow-Children Walk My Circles in the Snow* by Ray A. Young Bear.

SEVEN, vol. 2, no. 1: *Bone Yard* by Jim Barnes.

SOUTH DAKOTA REVIEW: *Tracking Rabbits: Night* by Jim Barnes; *Trains Made of Stone* and *Coming Back Home* by Ray A. Young Bear. Reprinted with permission of John Milton, editor.

WEST COAST POETRY REVIEW, Summer/Fall 1972: *Paiute Ponies* by Jim Barnes.

YARDBIRD READER, vol. 3, Frank Chin and Shawn Hsu Wong, eds.: *Forming Child Poems* by Simon Ortiz. Reprinted by permission of Yardbird Publishing Co., Berkeley, CA, 1975.

Contents

N. Scott Momaday   85

A Note on Contemporary
Native American Poetry

I take it that poetry is an expression of the human spirit. I have tried upon occasion to formulate a definition of the poem, and I have noted some of the definitions put forth by others. But it seems to me that in the final analysis the poem—that verbal equation which we commonly call by the name poetry—is perceptibly greater than any and all definitions of which I am aware. So it must be, I believe, with any art which exists for the sake of expressing the human spirit truly, for that spirit is itself a sum which is greater than its parts.

Contemporary Native American poetry proceeds from an older tradition than that which we think of as literature in the strict sense. Its roots run down into the very origins of language. We are accustomed to thinking of poetry as writing and to assume therefore that the origin and development of the poem is confined to the dimension of the written word. But this is of course a fallacy. In essence—and in substance—poetry existed long before the invention of the alphabet.

As it happens, contemporary Native American poetry—the poetry contained in this book, for example—is written, and it is written in English. It is by virtue of this fact committed to certain principles that are inherent in the English language and in the traditional forms of English verse. But this commitment reflects only one aspect of its character. There is at least another.

In order to understand the true impetus of contemporary Native American poetry, it is necessary to understand the nature of the oral tradition. Until quite recently the songs, charms, and prayers of the Native American—those things which we tend to think of as poetry, for want of a better term, perhaps—were embodied exclusively within the oral tradition; that is, their existence was wholly independent of writing. And so much of it remains, in the numerous Native American languages—unwritten languages—which survive to the present day. It is in the nature of the oral tradition that language is understood to be a vital and powerful thing in itself, creative in the deepest sense. It is the very element in which the life of the mind and spirit persists. Words, as they are carried on from one generation to another solely by means of the human voice, are sacred. Nothing is so potent as the word; nothing is so original or originative; and nothing is so close to beauty.

I mean to say that the oral tradition, which in some real measure informs the character of contemporary Native American poetry, is itself a reflection of certain fundamental attitudes with respect to language and therefore to literature, and that above all it is a reflection of man's persistent belief in the efficacy of words.

This is surely an idea which informs to one degree or another the poetry of all times and all places. But it seems to me especially relevant to contemporary Native American poetry, where it is perhaps closer than anything else in our time to the surface of human experience and the center of the human spirit.

N. Scott Momaday

Liz Sohappy Bahe

Liz Sohappy Bahe, a Yakima, was born in 1947 near Toppenish, Washington. Her Indian name is Omnama Cheshūts, which means Stopping On A Hill And Looking Down.

After spending her childhood in Washington, she attended high school at the Institute of American Indian Arts in Santa Fe, New Mexico. In the summer of 1970 she returned there to study in a post-graduate poetry workshop.

Since the fall of 1972, she has been living in Chinle, Arizona, with her husband and their two small sons.

Farewell

You sang round-dance songs.
I danced not to thundering drums
but to your voice singing.

You chiseled wood sculpture.
I watched not the tools or chips fly
but your strong hands carving.

You lived in a northern village.
I went there not to meet your people
but to walk where you had walked.

You followed calling drums.
I waited, willing the drums to stop.

Printed Words

I stared at the printed words
hazed, blurred, they became grey.
I trailed down the page
to a picture shouting what I read.

I thought about my people
up North—
far from here.
My land, the hot dry basin,
the pine on the mountain ranges
and the snowcapped peaks.

I thought of the killing word:
Civilization.
The steel buildings stabbing the earth,
stabbing old religions
now buried on the hilltop,
to have their tears drip black
from Industry's ash clouds.

I thought of the unseen tears
in eyes watching our valley
gashed by plows,
proud trees uprooted, dragged aside,
giving way to smothering tar roads.
And river veins pumped away
never knowing the path to the Columbia River.

I glanced at the blurring printed words
and felt an ancient anger swell,
bubble like a volcano in birth,
anger blackening the printed words
about your land being only a swamp
useless to Civilization.

I saw in a flash
the unknowing eyes of the Everglades—
alligators, egrets, water turkeys, ibises.
Animals I've never seen, never known
except from sadness that their fate lies
in printed words.

The words about the Everglades—
moist, mysterious, very much a land—
useless.
Words forgetting the animal people,
the Seminole, the Miccosukie,
who are standing in the way of the thing called
Civilization.

And What of Me?

Smoldering dry fern
hazes the oranges and reds
worn by the old people.

In strung beads
and smoked buckskin moccasins
they sit shoulder to shoulder
listening and watching.

In the tule and hemp woven lodge,
surrounded by feathered pine,
long canes thud, thud, thud;
men sob and women screech
old feather songs.

With muscles bulging,
a man holds his feather upright.
He sways and twirls
unable to free himself.

I, like the old people,
close my eyes
my mouth singing,
my mind shouting:
He has sinned—but what of me?

The feather is alive
as it jerks and turns
and the hand seeks to detach
itself, to reach for help,
to plead forgiveness.

And what of me,
I say sitting silently
knowing it is complete.

Sweat rolls down the man's face
as he lies on the earthen floor.
His trembling lips, his shaking body
are mine when the old people sing.

Revived by the brittleness
of boiled bitter-roots
the feather people and old people
sigh another year of life.

The fern smoke escapes
through an open tule mat:
but what of me?

The Ration Card

This ration card, once shocking pink,
was issued to me by a Blackfeet
at the tipi encampment
in Browning, Montana.

I don't remember the food,
but I feel the cold,
the slow winds brushing the Rockies,
breathing on me.

Dressed in buckskin and beads
I walked past design-painted tipis
to a huge tent where drums and bells battled—
uniting ancient war parties—
Paloos, Crows, Shoshones. . . .

I was not hungry for bread,
but I was not to refuse
another Indian's way of giving.

He smiled
as I signed my name
on his ration card.

I feel the burning of that day's sun
baking me a deeper hurting brown.
My hands' memory holds the hand-game bones,
one smooth, the other carved at center.

I waved
the bones as I scored
a stick.

My ration card will fade or be lost
but I feel last year's muses luring me
where emotions are rationed
in dance, in song, in that little taste.

Talking Designs

Cornhusk bag—
What is your story?
Other cornhusk bags tell of the weaver's life—
those stories traced by the old lady's fingers,
telling of tears, joy, birth, land of death.

Quilled buckskin—
Did Old Man whisper
the secret between porcupine quills and deer skin?
What story was in Old Man's fingers,
whispering secrets of desire, vanity, youth.

Beaded buckskin dress—
Is your story of me?
You were alone; I took and completed you
from moccasins to headband. . . .
Then I danced.
Now everyone notices you.
You are no longer alone.

Grandmother Sleeps

Ah! Grandmother weaves!
I watch her fingers
pull, grasp the twine
and cross the cornhusk.
When the sun is high, we eat.

Ah! Grandmother is beading!
I watch her trim fingers
pull, grasp the needle
as the beads lie side by side.
Night comes, grandmother sleeps.

Ah! Days pass, grandmother sleeps.
I will grasp her needle; her twine,
to bead and twine from dawn to dusk.
As grandmother lies on her tule mat,
I will wait for her to wake.

Once Again

Let go of the present and death.
Go to the place nearest the stars,
gather twigs, logs;
build a small fire;
a huge angry fire.

Gather nature's skin;
wet it; stretch it,
make a hard drum;
fill it with water
to muffle sound.

Gather dry leaves, herbs;
feed the fire.
Let the smoke rise
with the roundness of the sun.

Moisten your lips,
loosen your tongue,
let the chant echo
from desert, valley, and peak—
wherever home is.

Remember the smoke,
the chants, the drums,
the stick grandfather held
as he spoke in the dark
of his fathers' power.

Gather your memories
into a basket; into a pot;
into your cornhusk bag.
Your grandfather sings for us
beyond the dry rustling cornstalks.

Jim Barnes

Jim Barnes was born in eastern Oklahoma in 1933. He is of Choctaw descent. He moved to Oregon in 1951, where he worked for nearly ten years as a lumberjack. In 1960 he returned to Oklahoma to enroll at Southeastern State College, where he received his B.A. degree. He later earned his M.A. and Ph.D. from the University of Arkansas.

Barnes began writing seriously in the mid-fifties, but his first work wasn't published until 1968. Since then his poems have appeared in numerous literary magazines and journals. He is presently assistant professor of comparative literature at Northeast Missouri State University, in Kirksville, Missouri.

These Damned Trees Crouch

for W. D. Snodgrass

These damned trees crouch heavy under heaven.
As *I* crouch, if I talk, I often cuss
This confounded wood and my own soft heart.
Some hunters like this place and rise at seven
And stand in ease in weather like a lush;
Jim Barnes is crawling through the underbrush.

I don't know why I cannot find *my* house.
It ought to be around here somewhere. Fuss
And bother: the crooked tree, the skunk's art
Lingering on till dark to then arouse
All sleeping demons of the mighty bush;
Jim Barnes is crawling through the underbrush.

My name is just as common as a worm,
And derivative. If I could converse just
With something inside myself and know it
(Have a tête-à-tête with some small gentle germ),
I'd make a beeline home—that's where it starts.
Yes . . . most of all I'd like to be a poet.
But the wood is thick and won't allow old Herm
To come right winging down. I have to rush.
I have to find my house even though it hurts;
Jim Barnes is crawling through the underbrush.

Last Look at La Plata, Missouri

The park, the heart, you see at town's center is soft
underfoot. All winter long the dying bluegrass
has fed on cicada bones, enough to fill a loft:

the drone of dying, constant cymbals and hard bass,
recedes to a waning echo in your ear. Each year
the town drops an inch or two in the mud, and has

little sense of its going, though a certain fear
of losing trade caused The Palace to buy a shade
and paint the yellow open sign and sell kids beer.

The town speaks of history, and goes slightly mad.
The silver jet, the town's only hero's joke it's said,
has lost a tire; the fuselage and wing tanks, glad

for past skies, are captive to flung rocks and love-red
names. Summer was too long and heavy for the white
bandstand warping above lost chords and maidenheads.

The town affirms its past. The druggist kills his light
above the store. A diesel moans toward Kansas City.
A lone dog barks. A child cries. All of winter night.

Camping Out on Rainy Mountain

There is no confusion of objects in the eye,
but one *hill or* one *tree or* one *man.*

—N. *Scott Momaday,* House Made of Dawn

The grass bends: blades crack from a wind
reservation Indians forget to read.
The mountain is lean in light.
Something hard about this soil
makes you too mean to dream at night;
you bloat, but know you have a soul.

Why do you find yourself here?
You've looked better places, drunk beer
in Yuma till the melted roads oozed back,
tracked Bigfoot in Siuslaw snows.
But now all summer long you crack
your eyes on stone, count dead crows.

It's distance that holds you down, the dance
that's riding in the wind, the sense
of blue between you and the west.
Miles away a buzzard's wheeling up a sky.
You cup your hands above your eyes. You're blessed.
His shadow has missed you by a mile. Too high.

Tracking Rabbits: Night

The moon in your eyes is best.
Believe it:

light and shadows
stand distinct.

The thing to know
is how to blink

and keep tied to tracks
when the ground grows granite hard.

Take a parallel course: dead on. The tracks
are blue steel, and you are to catch the moon.

Beware long curves; never cut across.
A whistle will sometimes slow your prey.

When you are close you will have to
link up with his shadow,

pant with him,
stop with him,

snort at a crossing
he distrusts.

When he heads home
ride him into his steamy bed,

put your hot hands
on his dark hot head,

call him brother,
semblance, prey.

Bone Yard

A hundred buffalo
knee-deep in sludge.

Bones bleached to pebbles
and white sand.

No buzzard troubles
now to drop an eye
on long-spent bones
at this dried waterhole.

The land's cracked hide
speaks of thirst.
No tree lives.

Only the ghosts of hoofs
that still tramp along
play on a hot wind
which has no past.

Only in dead of winter
do the hoofs grow still,
when humped clouds
crowd low against the ground.

Sweating It Out on Winding Stair Mountain

for Carolyn Barnes

The roots around your soul and eyes
after too much bourbon twist sockets
sore. This mountain's too high to cry
sober on, the sky too wide to fill
a brain. Three crows are wheeling
up a peak. Caws crack thin air.
Sweat ices its way down your spine.

Last night love loomed as lonesome
as a timber wolf, the face a mask
you painted in your drunken dream.
What's real is that one white, brittle
moon you think you see pied against
the coldest blue a summer has known.

Nearly forty years and you've yet
to learn that love is measured by
the sun. There's no shade. The wind
pulls at your hair. The sky burns black
at sundown. You've got to go back down
before the crows laugh you straight to hell.

The Captive Stone

(at Heavener, Oklahoma)

Enmeshed in steel stands a stone,
near stunted ash and elm, cracked bones
of Yggdrasill, small trees of time:
the caged stone with ciphered runes
is part of Park where men once made
their mark with maul and biting bronze.

The aged stone, hard to hand's touch
when touch was still allowed,
has had its face forced clean:
lichen lies dead below washed runes;
webbed shadows of encircling steel
now mark time on the lone stone;
yet the stone stands as stone stood
when Odin still was king and came
with men to mark down lives and fates.

Now we who Sundays look long
on this stone's stark ruined face
see only stone and ciphered runes
under the steel's sharp shadows:
the whispering of wind through wire
carries scant legend, no hint of history.

Lying in a Yuma Saloon

Let them count scalps upon the barroom wall.
You'll lie yourself into some northern snow
and foxes fast with light and sage hens in their teeth.

This whiskey warms you clear to Yellowknife
when you try, to long dark winters' snows
you trapped silvers in for pelts and felt
their blood turn knifeblades back to faded flint.

Welcome to Yuma and bourbon in the bone
tell you late you'll never find your home
away from hills. The bar's a wreck
from last night's fight you were passed out in.

Salvation Army tambourines wring you dry
into another glass. Your eyes are full of black.
Your fist is jingling with bells of foxes' teeth,
and in your head lie snows no Apache sun has seen.

You wish the woman out the fractured door
and close your hands around a double Beam.
Let them all count scalps on the barroom wall.
Hell, you've known women who could eat a man alive,
and silvers on the loose not even frozen souls have seen.

Paiute Ponies

Silhouettes, they lean against a ringed moon,
their heads down against the threat of snow.
Below, a distant diesel moan runs
along the tracks, where dead coal cinders
gather frost, and plays out toward Winnemucca.

No movement. They hump against the night.
Only quivering patches of skin crack the air,
memories of a summer's fly.

Mane and tail hanging vertical as ice,
they sleep dead centuries,
or if ponies dream they dream.

Below on the flat where light strikes water,
a last ember sparks out. A dog complains.

The diesel warns again, begins its roar, passes.
They raise their heads like automatons, blink,
then drop once more into centuries or dreams.

Halcyon Days

Charlie Wolf used to whittle skinning knives
and swords from empty apple crates in winter.
He carved out blades I knew would never break,
true blades I knew instead would slice right through

any weed I chose to make a running deer
or any Rhode Island Red I chose to see
as enemy of God and man. Each old hen
knew my whoop meant feathers lost or worse

and squawked accordingly. Old Charlie used
to say that's why we got so many eggs
double-yolked—"scared the stuff right out of them
with that sword and that wild-eyed Choctaw yell."

Every sword I ever had before Charlie
drowned drunk on a coon hunt on the Arkansas
smelled of apples. Streaking round the barnyard
junk like a bullsnake after chicks, I breathed

pure Christmas before each ambush of red hens,
the white pine sword gleaming between my teeth.

Autobiography: Last Chapter

Coming in again, you know the town by boards it makes eyes touch,
   summer shirtsleeves worn long, heavy hats pulled down.

Always the wind stinks.

The woman you loved summers ago sits pale as bleached stones, her
   husband mad, their house a heap of broken bones.

The sky lies faded denim above your cousin's store; the false front
   from another age, dogeared as a tinhorn's wild joker, can't reflect
   your past in its cracked eye.

You want to cry, but know the sun turns tears to salt before they
   break from lids in this desperate town, where the only hope is a
   brittle Baptist bell banging sometimes Sundays.

You touch the woman by your side and want to explain the lack of
   paint away, but don't: she knows you are running back into
   yourself.

Joseph Bruchac

Joseph Bruchac was born in 1942 in Saratoga Springs, New York. His father's side of the family was Slovak immigrant, his mother's Abnaki. He was raised by his maternal grandfather.

Bruchac attended Cornell University where he intended to study conservation but ended up with a degree in creative writing and added to that an M.A. from Syracuse University.

After three years teaching in Ghana, he taught creative writing at Skidmore College and Comstock Prison and is the founder/editor of the *Greenfield Review*, a literary magazine. He has published two books of poetry, *Indian Mountain* (Ithaca House) and *The Buffalo in the Syracuse Zoo* (Greenfield Review Press) and is a recipient of grants from the New York State Creative Artist Program Service (CAPS) and the National Endowment for the Arts.

Bruchac lives in Greenfield Center, New York, with his wife and two sons.

The Grandmother Came Down to Visit Us

for Phil George

When the spider dropped down from the ceiling
Only Phil and I moved to save it
in a room full of people fearing
the shadow-weaver, the oldest gift giver.

We dropped it among suburban flowers
then went back in to get drunk,
finished every bottle in that house
to empty death
& then, full glasses of whiskey in our hands
& new bottles of wine in our pockets
we went back to the dormitory
where the workshop director
said to Phil
What's happened?
You were such a good Indian all week.

The grandmother came down
to visit us and they all want to hurt her
Phil said in his laughing voice
her web between our hands
as we left that house.

Elegy for Jack Bowman

This afternoon as I sat
on my grandfather's porch,
Thunderer's bolts crackling
across the close sky,
you lay in a room
where doctors tried in vain
to plug an aorta less strong
than your will to live
calmly and in love
with the land and the woman
you shared long life with.

As I closed my eyes,
hearing a heavy summer rain
and *He-noh*'s feet walking
across the heavens,
your eyes closed for a last time
thirty miles from this hill
where you and your brother
drove teams with lumber.

You were my grandfather
come to life again
when I saw you at his funeral
and in your face
which was his and your own
I read the stories
of logging and horses and knowing
how to fit the ground to plant.

You never lived more
than a step from the soil.
My last memory
is of you kneeling
to dig with your hands
new potatoes you'd planted.

Old Man, the last of my old men.

Stone Giant

While breaking the big rock
frost tides raised like the
boneshattered rib of a buried giant
a piece of stone burst off like shrapnel
to strike my shoulder
& I stopped, covered with earth
what was left.

Now, half a moon later
the scar stands there
like the smallpox charm
etched into my other limb
and some nights I wake
certain that in my dream
I've been flying through earth
slow as the tide
that moves great stones.

Frozen Hands

Lifting my fingers
from the blue metal of the gun
is like peeling a bandaid
from a partly healed wound
bits of white skin
remain on the barrel

turning my hands
i see the light
beneath the flesh

with each breath
the air wraps about me
weaving a tight
cocoon of blue ice

i move suddenly
and leave a man of skin
caught in the December wind.

Three Poems for the Indian Steelworkers in a Bar Where I Used to Drink

I

This place is cold
as the soul of a hundred winters
bottles glitter from tables
bright as markers of polished marble

My greeting lifts the faces of my friends
like furrows of dark soil
turned by a plow to fall again
& I have only come in to
be out of the winter night

There are no songs we can teach each other

But John Last-Walking-Bear
holds a lantern wavering before my eyes
it brightens the dark corners
Tilting it slightly he ripples
effervescent light into our glasses

II

These days I drink in another bar
Only the young and beautiful come here
They toss their long hair
with the lovely abandon of horses
They can walk out into the streets
They can return to familiar houses
not washed away by the river of a hundred years
& when they sleep their bodies float
above their beds, light as Ariel

III

Driving home at night
through the Onondaga Reservation
headlights strike empty white fields
& tired houses with back broken roofs

At the bend in the road are the hills
the Holder Up of the Heavens dropped
on the Stone Giants

& I remember
that this is a land
which has been bright with magic

Hiking

A man who loves hiking
must be glad to move on.
I have never been one of those
though I have lived all my life
by one road or another.

And had I been in that glen
when the doe gave birth
to twin fawns,
travellers coming by
a hundred years from then
might have found me,
roots deep in the ferns,
an old birch tree.

City

There are seeds within the tide
Unmarked by season
rainbows of oil
the glitter of metal
and in soft crepe decay
fish are sinking

Wind touches the roof
of the bay
Snow bursts
into icy leaves
The mouth of the river
turns into smoke
and becomes the city

IV

There is a stream which rises
halfway down that mountain
My father showed it to me,
place he found in a dream,
the withered spirit of an old Indian
leading him like a wisp of fog
to its banks
I shall go to that last water
when I am old
and my blood runs
like the sad Hudson river
heavy with the waste
of civilization
I shall go there
and wade into those clear ripples
where the sandy bottom
is spread with stones
which look like the bones
of beautiful ancient animals
I shall spread my arms
in the sweet water
and go like a last wash of snow
down to the loon meadow
in the last days of April

Coming Back

When they woke me
tangled in their blue nets
the worm holes in my hands were gone

a bright painted boat
danced in the water
like a tethered colt

apparently
i had learned something
for i did not ask them why
or who i was
but stood
touched their hands and foreheads
and began to walk
up the golden sword's arc of sand

now
a thousand years
and two continents away
you wonder why my feet
move in dance to a distant drum

Second Skins—A Peyote Song

I

Fox woman
dances, string of blue beads
at her waist
her hands are open
offer you a dream

II

Drum
asks no one to listen
speaks no words
but is there
in the blood
dark strong
lightless surge
in veins
the drum sounds
heart answers
If you are still alive
your feet have been dancing
long before you thought
you heard this song

III

Gull woman
turns in the wind
she wears the grey coat
of feathers and wind
behind the lids of her closed eyes
you are turning in the wind

For a Winnebago Brave

Nighthawks circle
through the midwestern elms
& White Rabbit (his name on
a social security card)
tries to brag of twenty-two feathers
in a room full of stony freaks
who wish to catch his soul
with questions about Nam.

He speaks in Winnebago &
they answer in German.
I'm Sioux, man, he says
and crooks a hand as if
to smash an African fertility
carving, pulls out his two knives
& the joint circles the room.
They do not understand warriors.

I threw my silver stars into
the river, he says
& tries to brag of twenty-two feathers,
his skinny body caught
in the overstuffed chair
like a dragonfly in a spider's web.
In this room full of shadows
it seems that a bird of light
hides beneath his dark blemished skin
and must beat its wings
or die of a broken heart.

Poem for Jan

Seeking the words
    as wings seek the lift of a wind
    the thought of your laughter
    to lift me over the rooftops. . .

But you drift away
    with the long ago summer
and I stand here, getting older
awkward as a wading heron
    forever looking back
    over his stooped shoulder

For Joseph Bruchac

For Gladys Cardiff

Gladys Cardiff

Gladys Cardiff was born in Browning, Montana, in 1942. She is part Cherokee of the North Carolina Owl Family. She attended the University of Washington where she studied with Theodore Roethke, Vernon Watkins and Nelson Bentley. She has given numerous poetry readings under the auspices of the Seattle Public Library Poetry Series and at the University of Washington.

She is currently teaching in the Poetry in the Schools Program run by the Washington State Arts Commission and living in Edmonds, Washington, with her husband and two children.

Leaves Like Fish

Cottonwood, willow, and briar,
Night air billows in the dark grove,
Hauls the alders over, their leaves

Jumping, spilling silver-bellied on the lawn;
The lighted wind is running with a flood
Of green fish, phosphorescent and wild

On the winter grass, breaking like struck matches,
Without warmth or place, random as green minnows.
Above the clouds the sky waits, one-celled,

Expanded over tides and winds, loving
The south wind as much as the north,
Schooling the planets in discretion and form.

Tlanusi' yi, the Leech Place

Surely it is death to come here.
This overhang of rock
opens a shadowy well in the river
to give me a deep look.
I am hungry for fish.
I forget the woman tossed up
downstream,
her face without nose or ears.
I never saw
the baby that disappeared,
the quiet sleeper.
"I'll tie red leech skins upon my legs
and wear them for garters."
My song scythes over wet fields,
parting the water like braids
wound with foam feathers,
wound with sunperches, snakes, and green turtles.
"I'll tie red leech skins upon my legs
and wear them for garters."
Its breath is like milk.
Young as I am, I am
Old in striped *ahunwogi,*
Girdled in red and in water.
Young as I am I know
The secret caverns in the Hiwassee,
That the river is eating the land.
I was hungry for fish.
I was from Birdtown.
I am dressed in a whirlpool of leech skins,
I am no more.

Long Person

Dark as wells, his eyes
Tell nothing. They look
Out from the print with small regard
For this occasion.
Dressed in neat black, he sits
On a folded newspaper
On a sawhorse in front of his blacksmith shop.
Wearing a black suit and white, round-brimmed hat,
My father stands on one side, his boy face
Round and serious. His brother stands
Like a reflection on the other side.
They each hold a light grasp on the edge
Of their daddy's shoulder, their fingernails
Gleaming like tiny moons on the black wool.
Each points his thumb up at the sky,
As if holding him too closely, with their whole hand,
Would spur those eyes into statement.
Coming out of a depth known as dream—
Or is it memory?
I can see inside the door where the dim shapes
Of bellows and tongs, rings and ropes hang on the wall,
The place for fire, the floating anvil,
Snakes of railroad steel, wheels in heaps,
Piled like turtles in the dark corners.
Long Person, you passed a stone's throw away from his door,
Your ripples are Cherokee prayers,
You carry the hopes of this nation within your banks,
You and he are alike, you are contained histories,
You are a generation of yet unbroken channels.

Combing

Bending, I bow my head
And lay my hands upon
Her hair, combing, and think
How women do this for
Each other. My daughter's hair
Curls against the comb,
Wet and fragrant—orange
Parings. Her face, downcast,
Is quiet for one so young.

I take her place. Beneath
My mother's hands I feel
The braids drawn up tight
As a piano wire and singing,
Vinegar-rinsed. Sitting
Before the oven I hear
The orange coils tick
The early hour before school.

She combed her grandmother
Mathilda's hair using
A comb made out of bone.
Mathilda rocked her oak wood
Chair, her face downcast,
Intent on tearing rags
In strips to braid a cotton
Rug from bits of orange
And brown. A simple act,

Preparing hair. Something
Women do for each other,
Plaiting the generations.

Dragon Skate

What sound awoke me?
The grate of shells?
But I am not in the sea.
Who is there?
Do you know me?
One who knew me is dead.
The hag that took me from the beach is dead.
She took me,
Yanked my head back, and
My pectorals like broken wings, and
The plate of my body, and
My whip,
All of me distorted
In an s for sorcery.
I curled to a wizened dragon, brown as a scab,
On her drying rack.

Is this daylight foaming, ah flooding, my eye holes
Red, red?
I'm tight as a gut string.

Before her,
I moved, easy
Over the ocean's crust,
Undulating,
Mesozoic,
Swilling on mollusks,
Loving the sea bottom, myself
An ovoid kiss.
She
Kissed the backside of Satan.
Did her bones jig

Under the howling strappado,
Or does she,
Does she lie flat?
She buried me alive, the witch,
Trying to hide herself inside boxes, in dark corners,
In ashes.
And I, in agony
While the years gathered like silt in the cave of my face,
Waited,
Changed in this scorched bandage of a body.

Yet?
Are you there?
I arose from black fire.
I could move again.
Let me show you.
Why do you wait?
Lift me! Lift me!

Carious Exposure

Your eyes are open.
Three A.M. you are staring at me.
The vision behind that stare
Has nothing to do with my
Returned look,
Like the patients who come to you
Tonight you wear
A trusting, hurt expression.
As if—what? all you know
Has bullied you into depression?
I would relieve your pain,
Massage your neck and feet,
Or better, do like you,
Extract or mend what hurts.
I am gentle for this time,
Covering my probings, as you do,
With quiet conversation.

To Frighten a Storm

(A Cherokee Incantation)

O now you come in rut
In rank and black desire,
To beat the brush, to lash
The wind with your long hair.
Ha! I am afraid,
Exceedingly afraid.
But see? Her path goes there,
Along the swaying tops
Of trees, up to the hills.
Too long she is alone.
Bypass our fields, and mount
Your ravages of fire
And rain on higher trails.
You shall have her lying down
Upon the smoking mountains.

Swimmer

Speaking like wind,
Swimmer says,
"He who wears bells,"
the Thunder's necklace,
most sacred snake,
uncoils in a stream of yellow
arrowheads.
Sge'. Listen.
He gives his sons
the she-bear's song,
"*Tsa gi, tsa gi, hwi lahi,*
When you hear the hunter come down,
upstream, upstream you go."
Outside the steaming *asi*
Uguku calls,
searching for a dark place to hide
his burned eyes.
Rattlesnake, bear, and owl
show this man the center,
where their voices rise
as smoke from blue mountain.

Grey Woman

A woman coming down the snowy road
In moccasins, a basket on her arm,
Her back bent by ninety Indian winters,
To pick inside the garbage bins below
The porches of the Cheyenne reservation,
A well-known personage among her people

Called Grey Woman. Finding a tin of sour
Butter, she makes her way between the lines
Of sheets that hang in rigid squares;
    each step
Dependent on a frame less surely pinned
Than frozen cloth cold-soldered to a wire.
She takes a rancid gob to eat when once

The red Wyoming sun fell to her feet.
Young when the young men reeled, tied
    to the sun
And bringing it down, she watched one
    dance alone
On thongs sewn in his chest, his breath
    in blasts
That shook the twirling feathers on
    his pipe.
She hears the echo in her chirping heart,
The sound of day outlasted. The night
    she died,
Following the old belief, all doors
    were locked
Until, after the manner of her ancestors,
She found *Maheo* and a final place.
The hand has turned to horn, and obdurate
Her spirit stands unhoused before my door.

Lance Henson

Lance Henson, a Cheyenne from Calumet, Oklahoma, was born in 1944. He served in the U.S. Marine Corps and is a graduate of the Oklahoma College of Liberal Arts in Chickasha. He is a member of the Cheyenne Dog Soldier Society and belongs to the Native American Church. He is currently enrolled in Tulsa University's Graduate Creative Writing Program.

Henson has published a book, *Keeper of Arrows: Poems for the Cheyenne* and recently has completed a series of poems for inclusion in a Cheyenne/Arapaho cultural textbook to be published by Oklahoma University Press. He is at work on a novel and several poems to be published in an anthology of writings by Vietnam veterans.

Our Smoke Has Gone Four Ways

our smoke has gone four ways
it calls for us

my brothers smile with tears
we may never meet again

eagle of fire whose
wings are scented cedar

moon of forever who
guards the sacred seed

keep us strong
to meet the
coming days.

Dawn in January

end of a long stillness
like some name finally
found
i have known you forever

as this portion of winter
sings through the motion
of dawn
i listen as a child to the
lute far away
whose song
vague as the face of a
long dead
voice

whispers to
me

Last Words, 1968

you said it went all the way
a kind of river into a kind
of sea

you said it and went away
your legacy
a smoking rubble of ashen
dreams

there is nothing of your words
among the garden graves alone
flies carry themselves into
the screen

come back

i am ready to begin again

Grandfather

the visions you never saw
still deliver me from the void

you stay now
beyond
where the snow is
no longer pain

wait for me   wait for me

i will follow

The Cold

what remains of summer
is hidden in the memories
of crows

in our sleep their shadows
inherit us
we pass warm ashes
of ourselves

we sit on the cold mountain
among the lonely wolves

Moon at Three a.m.

i am scorned by patterns which hold
me inconsistently
between the hours of candles half burnt

and the memory of flowers
resembling bones wrapped
in quiet
                  guiltless
                        sleep

Wish

somewhere
a niche
a morning of
dusk

where you

voice

repeat the only
word you know

Roberta Hill

Roberta Hill, an Oneida, was born February 17, 1947 in Baraboo, Wisconsin. She attended the University of Wisconsin, from which she graduated with a B.A. in psychology, and the University of Montana, from which she received an M.F.A. in writing.

She has been a Poet in Residence for the Poets in the Schools Program in St. Paul, Minnesota, and currently teaches at Sinte Gleska College in Rosebud, South Dakota. Her poems have appeared in *American Poetry Review*, *Poetry Northwest*, *Southern Review*, and others.

She lives in Rosebud, South Dakota, with her husband and young son, Jacob.

Night along the Mackinac Bridge

I wait to tangle fear around my hand
like fire, to hold your owl's eyes with mine.
Lake Michigan dries sweat from magic,
squeezes belief into the world. Jacob runs
away the night as beer crackles down his jeans.
My past rustles offshore, a sail only rowboats watch.

I return to kin I've avoided fifteen years,
and find my skin's never felt so much at home.
That cinnamon wrapping would tear
from schools where Jesuits waged revenge.
Near Oneida, geese gather over fields, fewer now
bound for Labrador. Last year, you left with them.

I'll unravel black hair, shape mongoloid folds,
always be stupid about the songs. Like a miller
burned by bulbs, I remember stillness
behind the faded blind, a light that hummed
my shoulders into fire. What was once so distant
breaks upon me now, while dark water crumbles the moon.

Direction

Walk east. Dawn polishes the sky,
turning frost to rainbows, vapor.
A fever, alien and wild, is in me,
like slivers, cut loose from the sun's core,
flow in my fingers, ease in my eyes.
The sun leaves light under trees,
circle on circle, drop on drop. Pine moths
suckle daisies to light up mountain slopes.

I saw your picture, and let aches surrender
to the avalanche. This place holds the memory
of rocking. Slow, white curtains breathe in gusts.
Flowery songs hummed lazily out of tune.
The sky changed, I've become a stranger
hating sloven clocks and vacant pain.

In the south, heat lashes you to cherries. I chronicle
the sun as it burns jewel-like reflections between leaves,
as it flares into air this wavering smell of camomile.
Smoke drifts along peonies, wet, ant-seeded,
and rests in lilacs rubbed with blue sky. I would be content
as a gull watching waves bend light into dark.

In the threshing wind, a gate swings.
Bones were never meant for one like her. Terrible red eye
at every doorstep. Circled sunlight
cups the trees. A misty heron flies along the pine,
she's the reason I've come. Mountains hush
my dull sense, hush the deep-throated ache, uneasy trees.

A father is cigarette smoke late on winter nights,
tears on a weather-tender face,
a smell of earth and powder.
The piano and violin lonely, and the artist gone,
she slipped into the blue painting
where a dwarf hides in the clouds.
Like you, I wait first light to strike
darkness. In north air, the mazes twist repeatedly,
perfection never rests. To find a lost tradition,
I would watch your heart for signs
cracklings in a pine,
footsteps on a marsh floor.

Our closets held the scent of loss,
and clothes for a woman no longer needy.
But the rocking I hold true
though it often robs my heart.
The rocks from the man in the French Sudan,
the quartz and mica dissolved with kaleidoscopes.
Snow patterns in red and blue,
broken into, scattered on a rug,
like stories for a child's idle years.

The moon leans west. Blurred by trees, she clings
to grey rock and grass in patches.
Small long cloud slung over low mountain.
Dreams gather in these mists. I've lived
as a misshapen thing, bound by water and geese
in flight. Lights flicker up hard against bald stone.
No music lilts my stifling home. I live here
unafraid of storms. No music, just rain,
this thunder, growing.

Falling Moon

Reach for arrows of falling light. A man once sang
in this temple. The moon stretched out
her richest dreams to him, softly touching
the faces of his people. Eyes of dark blood.
Hands like warm adobe.
Cedars drink thin air.
Ruins are left to us walking the paths of rain,
following where
shadows meet and listen.

They piled the even bricks to echo the moon's pale ring.
When she rose, whistling like a doe
in the quiet glare,
some would enter these dens, the deep rooms of wolves,
purer than we could wish,
without the weight of bodies.
What have we left? Secrets of dust and hate.
Below this rim world,
the earth fades like a prayer.

We wear stranger masks.
Seven miles from Porcupine
tanks chill the prairie. Flares bloom
in thunderheads to fall like flickering comets.
A boy crouches in dirt. He has held the sun.
Its hard gold fire breathes with him. *Minneconjous* fell
like snow. Sparkling water people.
Death will hum like ashes in their ears.
The stillness branches.

Deep inside the noise of burning comes
the sound of wings. When hawks die
singing, some hidden vein will burst inside my throat,
dreams will shiver on this haunted sleep.
Reach for arrows of rising light.
Bones flash like shells
in salt green grass.
A thin moon soars above the pines,
plants no blame in open fields.

I watch a weeping birch let its trail of leaves
ride a stalking wind.
Owls call through the haze.
How can I mark this sorrow? We live the flames
of twilight. Dewclaws drum the trappings of this dust.
Meeting canyons still hold blood and flesh.
Spirits rise on blackmouthed water, dance like grouse
in dry creek beds. Believe the distant ice,
the robber storm.

Inside the circled weeds, raw hours strike. Purple thistles
wrinkle near the corn.
Cottonwoods will answer
when they come to make the grey mare captive
in her flight.
I keep hearing singing in the sun.
It rustles through the turnips on those hills.
Crows will find us walking north.
You and I must gather under elms.

A Nation Wrapped in Stone

for Susan Iron Shell

When night shadows slipped across the plain, I saw a man
beside his horse, sleeping where neither man nor horse
had been. I've prayed
to a star that lied. The spirits near the ceiling of your room,
did they leave on horseback, turning dew into threads
by moonlight?
In wild stretch of days, you didn't fear ashes or weeping.
We, left behind, can't warn sunlight.
Isaac, you left with the wind.

The chokecherry grows slower. I held your trembling wife,
and windows trembled in our north room. The creek gnaws
remaining snow. Our blood runs pale.
You taught us to be kind to one another. Now we wake, questioning
our dreams. Nighthawks in warm fog. A nation wrapped in stone.
What do nurses
know of hay, of scents that float broken between canyons,
of strength in a worn face? You wept love, not death.
Around your bed, owls stood.

The north wind hunts us with music, enough pain
to set fires in ancient hills. West winds growl
around Parmalee.
The tanned, uneven banks will hold more frost. Unlike dust
we cannot die from tears. You've settled
on a quiet prairie. Shrouded eyes
in thickets give a reason to contain
this heavy rind. We are left with grief, sinking boneward,
and time to watch rain soak the trees.

Sleeping with Foxes

You burst into the world with smiles wide as April,
a crimsom baby, blossoming, called Rosa.
They drenched you, not knowing it dwarfed Indian magic,
and you were blessed with names of flowers, saints. Dad's guitar
rusted near toys. You, a red-brown nugget among sparrows,
ran to touch azaleas, Lou'siana tenderness,
and chased chickens during hurricanes.

When you were ten, the neighbor boys tied, burned a savage.
Mother pulled you, crying, from the flame.
On the shaker porch, when spring rain whipped
trees, we philosophized as children
about drops caught in our eyrie. Small eagles,
one in blue flannel, longing for leaden wind and pride.
Lady who no longer lives with time,
listen, take this ragged shawl, this dew.

The years have swung roughly since you left Denver.
Stones anchor these mountains.
Where or how can I reach you?
I've checked mail from Lake Tahoe
and points east, asked detectives
who confessed you were a bride, a bone.
Are you sleeping with foxes, nosedeep in warmth,
buried in thickets of blackberries and ground fog?

Wind blows the marshgrass along the bay shore.
Bees twist honeysuckle in our backyard.
It is we who have grown desperate, bitter,
sensing that wind blows in gusts, skims
this jagged distance without leaving sons.

Beginning the Year at Rosebud, S.D.

No pavement chalks the plain with memories,
rows of curb crumbling to dirt each twilight.
Raw bones bend from an amber flood of gravel,
used clothing, whiskey. We walked, and a dead dog
seemed to leap from an iced shore, barks swelling her belly.
Three days I've waited, eyes frosted shut
to illusions of scrap and promising wind.

I'm untrapped here, in another place where the banister
interned my smile and glued my soul to the lion's mane,
walls nibble this new year. While cedar cradles
its medicine in ironing, I see my father's red eyes lock
thunder in the living room. Someone's brain cries in the basket,
watches steam and church bells fade. My empty hands ache
from stains and cigarette smoke. I am a renegade,
name frozen at birth, entrails layered with scorpions.

Hay fields have poisoned my ears by now.
The fourth day grows heavy and fat like an orchid.
A withered grandmother's face trickles wisdom
of buffalo wallows and graveyards marked
with clumps of sage. Here, stars are ringed
by bitter wind and silence. I know of a lodestone in the prairie,
where children are unconsoled by wishes,
where tears salt bread.

For Lance Henson

For Roberta Hill

Dream of Rebirth

We stand on the edge of wounds, hugging canned meat,
waiting for owls to come grind
nightsmell in our ears. Over fields,
darkness has been rumbling. Crows gather.
Our luxuries are hatred. Grief. Worn-out hands
carry the pale remains of forgotten murders.
If I could only lull or change this slow hunger,
this midnight swollen four hundred years.

Groping within us are cries yet unheard.
We are born with cobwebs in our mouths
bleeding with prophecies.
Yet within this interior, a spirit kindles
moonlight glittering deep into the sea.
These seeds take root in the hush
of dusk. Songs, a thin echo, heal the salted marsh,
and yield visions untrembling in our grip.

I dreamed an absolute silence birds had fled.
The sun, a meagre hope, again was sacred.
We need to be purified by fury.
Once more eagles will restore our prayers.
We'll forget the strangeness of your pity.
Some will anoint the graves with pollen.
Some of us may wake unashamed.
Some will rise that clear morning like the swallows.

Lines for Marking Time

Women know how to wait here.
They smell dust on wind and know you haven't come.
I've grown lean walking along dirt roads,
under a glassy sun, whispering to steps.
Twenty years I've lived on ruin. When I escaped
they buried you. All that's left is a radio
with a golden band. It smells of heat,
old baseball games, a shimmering city inside.
The front door has stopped banging and the apple tree
holds an old tire strange children swing in.

This house with broken light has lost me
now when the sweet grass dries. Its scent lingers
in the living room among sewing and worn-out shoes.
In your silence, I grew visions for myself, and received
a name no one could live up to. Blood rises
on hot summer wind, rose petals trickle
past rough solemn wood. Hear the distant sobbing?
An Indian who's afraid of tears. She charms her eyes
to smiling, waits for the new blue star. Answers
never come late.

Look west long enough, the moon will grow
inside you. Coyote hears her song, he'll teach you now.
Mirrors follow trails of blood and lightning.
Mother needs the strength of one like you. Let blood
dry, but seize the lightning. Hold it like your mother
rocks the trees. In your fear, watch the road, breathe deeply.
Indians know how to wait.

Star Quilt

These are notes to lightning in my bedroom.
A star forged from linen thread and patches.
Purple, yellow, red like diamond suckers, children

of the star gleam on sweaty nights. The quilt unfolds
against sheets, moving, warm clouds of Chinook.
It covers my cuts, my red birch clusters under pine.

Under it your mouth begins a legend,
and wide as the plain, I hope Wisconsin marshes
promise your caress. The candle locks

us in forest smells, your cheek tattered
by shadow. Sweetened by wings, my mothlike heart
flies nightly among geraniums.

We know of land that looks lonely,
but isn't, of beef with hides of velveteen,
of sorrow, an eddy in blood.

Star quilt, sewn from dawn light by fingers
of flint, take away those touches
meant for noisier skins,

anoint us with grass and twilight air,
so we may embrace, two bitter roots
pushing back into the dust.

Song for Healing

Mary, will you ever grow? Water, blessed by bishops
has been poured on your head and even the sea has tried.
How was I to know those sixth grade friends were queer.
Two strange girls but neighbors just the same.
All the inane smiles that lead from gradeschool
toward the blurred leap, dusty feet you have to trample
midnight dread. The camel that you called yourself
longed for rain and straps to hold its anger down.
Camel anger, being left by father,
the theft of any scrap of hope.

No dungeons are at Winnebago. There's light, air
and padlocked doors. The women haven't changed
a thousand years. Day-glow eyes flower into shrieks
in this Thorazine Age. Tumbling down the hall,
sixth grade again, without your camel's hump of hate,
I feel like a mother, a childhood friend. Outside, a wobbly
young bird flies from a stump. The warm mud oozes raw.
Madness is winter and solitary. You gag on memories
and guilt, 'til it smashes you down to hunks of church window,
a spectrum of holy trips to the sea.

Mary, will you ever grow again? Be old as lichen on bark
or rock? Insanity's a jewel that keeps the owner
bold in any wind. Remember mommy foaming at the mouth?
Your brightness dissolves by fury into a snail's breath.
The apocalypse of soul echoes in eyes hollow in fright.
Your tongue keeps absolving teeth devoid of prayer.
Don't let life roll out its victories like coins. Become
some lady in a flower print dress, children laughing on the way
to school. Come to day, from your incandescent dawn.
Live in a happy anonymous town, your lawn,
green, your hair, a bit grey.

Whispers

for Tony

They will come for you in morning
where faded rooms mask the taste of bones.
Birds flit then rise over low bushes
that twist rootlike along slopes. A morning like others,
touched with bacon smell, worn leaves,
and air so sharp it freezes eyes into clear vision.
They will come to say I am not blessed
or loved, that all I own is worthless. Soapstone carved
in delicate designs without concern or meaning, strands of hair
locked in pony beads, a feather cut by messages and time.

Your destiny trails the purple star, Antares.
Few moons win us, wrap around our souls. Your fingers
slip my grasp, the touch branches give the wind.
In softening years, the wheel will creak
but never stop. The moon on my thumbnail
sets. Birth is never easy, seeds break
with their own lost art. In your turning, remember turnips
softly thawing on the plain, a canyon with its river partner,
the strong trail and ashes. Watch the rinsed sky, Tony,
the night when stars own wings.

They will come for you in evening
from a place where dust is cloaked. I will watch
the moon discovering her face. We'll speak of stone, seashine
and hide the words that guide us, the songs that heal us,
the last language unopen to easy fear. In that moment,
my life will be a package. In that dusk,
the final stillness, sweet. The ants return seeking
weeds and pearls. And I will wait, soundless and unwakened.
All footsteps harmless, all secrets dampened I will wait,
to see that storm of riches in your sudden gaze.

Midnight on Front Street

"Peacock colored tears and rotten oranges,"
said the fire. "You swim in salt and think
it is the sea." Thief, webs like crowns keep us
near this door. You laugh. One hundred voices answer,
"No migration." You act the warrior, wind thief,
yet watchers from shade declare your sky stormless.
By whose right do you court exhausting thunder
bound in leaves?
Whose night rocks do you drown like mossy turtles?
I shelter with claws one final whisper.
Ashes for a tired moon.

Once *Mosquito* sang in swamps
on the far moon rim. Green flanks bridged the silence
with music. A thief hidden in the clouds,
hacked his tail, a sea sound thundered,
hacked his wings, rustling trees broke,
smashed the flanks. The silent dust boiled
into mountain, forest. Birds flooded from his head.
Animals ran from mouth or ear. The legs
jumped stiffly on the grass. Shells cracked.
Each one a man. Granite. Each a nation.
The fire steams and spits. Look skyward,
my fingers curl.

The eaglebone cries. My lair mushrooms.
Seven echoes fell the walls. Across glaring fields,
light sweeps in a rush of stars. Notes burn
on an empty rise. In Wyoming,
she howled and dark plains drank up rainbows.
I rub my arms with magic stones.
Call nets down, down into mud,

hunt for other thieves. My rooms fill with frost,
and snarled roots. Haze around a streetlight grows.
I must wait. In the mirror a woman
is answering sleep. Elms bend against the night.

In the Madison Zoo

No rooster wakes them. A donkey brays
in blue dawn air. She never sleeps.
Lake Wingra snares the lilies,
hurries the morning star. The white down
of her talons sheds the city heat.
Far more terrible than lions, smooth pain stone
I cannot leave. A Kodiak in peanuts, paper,
thinks of seals from a long past hunger.
Sky like first day ice. White wings
for bitter ambush, stiff and rimmed with iron.
When she hoots, hide hands in pockets. Such luck
will tear down cobwebs near the stars. What thin bone
rings when I see you, Owl? Waterbugs dream
in knots and whirlpools. I hear music
from railroad evenings.
Town lights blink through the leaves.

Somewhere a fire brightens on the plain.
In the big oak behind the house, amber eyes
crowd my rooms. She hums, while her dress
wraps its tattered edge around the trunk. Arrogant, wise,
she calls me out from this dusty window where voices
try to hold the cup and saucer still.
Sparrow-bound to rain, I remember a cage
under younger trees.

There the cottonwoods rattle and thirst.
She's the only light in tunnelled black.
If I were to leave, my house would burn.
They would find me thrashing in the weeds
with a face of sand. Changed by a glance,
I haunt the fierce wet hills, press the granite roots
to reach a sound, rich as thunder,
bright and fleeting as the path of a snail.

N. Scott Momaday

N. Scott Momaday, a Kiowa, was born in Lawton, Oklahoma in 1934. He grew up on various Southwestern reservations and was educated at Indian schools. He received his B.A. from the University of New Mexico and his M.A. and Ph.D. from Stanford University. He has taught English at the University of California at Santa Barbara and at Berkeley and was a Stanford Creative Writing Fellow in Poetry and a Guggenheim Fellow. His first novel, *House Made of Dawn* (Harper & Row), received the Pulitzer Prize for Fiction in 1969 and has been made into a film. He is also the author of *Angle of Geese and Other Poems* (Godine) and *The Way to Rainy Mountain* (University of New Mexico Press), the story of the migration of the Kiowa people from northern Montana to the southern Plains. Momaday is currently professor of English and Comparative Literature at Stanford University.

Carriers of the Dream Wheel

This is the Wheel of Dreams
Which is carried on their voices,
By means of which their voices turn
And center upon being.
It encircles the First World,
This powerful wheel.
They shape their songs upon the wheel
And spin the names of the earth and sky,
The aboriginal names.
They are old men, or men
Who are old in their voices,
And they carry the wheel among the camps,
Saying: Come, come,
Let us tell the old stories,
Let us sing the sacred songs.

Forms of the Earth at Abiquiu

for Georgia O'Keefe

I imagine the time of our meeting
There among the forms of the earth at Abiquiu,
And other times that followed from the one—
An easy conjugation of stories,
And late luncheons of wine and cheese.
All around there were beautiful objects,
Clean and precise in their beauty, like bone.
Indeed, bone: a snake in the filaments of bone,
The skulls of cows and sheep;
And the many smooth stones in the window,
In the flat winter light, were beautiful.
I wanted to feel the sun in the stones—
The ashen, far-flung winter sun—
But this I did not tell you, I believe,
But I believe that after all you knew.
And then, in those days, too,
I made you the gift of a small, brown stone,
And you described it with the tips of your fingers
And knew at once that it was beautiful—
At once, accordingly you knew,
As you knew the forms of the earth at Abiquiu:
That time involves them and they bear away,
Beautiful, various, remote,
In failing light, and the coming of cold.

The Delight Song of Tsoai-Talee

I am a feather on the bright sky
I am the blue horse that runs in the plain
I am the fish that rolls, shining, in the water
I am the shadow that follows a child
I am the evening light, the lustre of meadows
I am an eagle playing with the wind
I am a cluster of bright beads
I am the farthest star
I am the cold of the dawn
I am the roaring of the rain
I am the glitter on the crust of the snow
I am the long track of the moon in a lake
I am a flame of four colors
I am a deer standing away in the dusk
I am a field of sumac and the pomme blanche
I am an angle of geese in the winter sky
I am the hunger of a young wolf
I am the whole dream of these things

You see, I am alive, I am alive
I stand in good relation to the earth
I stand in good relation to the gods
I stand in good relation to all that is beautiful
I stand in good relation to the daughter of *Tsen-tainte*
You see, I am alive, I am alive

Wide Empty Landscape
with a Death in the Foreground

Here are weeds about his mouth;
His teeth are ashes.

It is this which succeeds him:
This huge, barren plain.

For him there is no question
Of elsewhere. His place

Is just this reality,
This deep element.

Now that he is dead he bears
Upon the vision

Merely, without resistance.
Death displaces him

No more than life displaced him;
He was always here.

The Bear

What ruse of vision,
escarping the wall of leaves,
    rending incision
into countless surfaces,

    would cull and color
his somnolence, whose old age
    has outworn valor,
all but the fact of courage?

    Seen, he does not come,
move, but seems forever there,
    dimensionless, dumb,
in the windless noon's hot glare.

    More scarred than others
these years since the trap maimed him,
    pain slants his withers,
drawing up the crooked limb.

    Then he is gone, whole,
without urgency, from sight,
    as buzzards control,
imperceptibly, their flight.

To a Child Running with Outstretched Arms in Canyon de Chelly

You are small and intense
In your excitement, whole,
Embodied in delight.
The backdrop is immense;

The sand drifts break and roll
Through cleavages of light
And shadow. You embrace
The spirit of this place.

Winter Holding Off the Coast of North America

This dread is like a calm,
And colorless. Nothing
Lies in the stricken palm
But the dead cold coming.

Out there, beyond the floes,
On the thin, pewter plane,
The polar currents close,
And stiffen, and remain.

The Gourd Dancer

Mammedaty, 1880–1932

I. The Omen

Another season centers on this place.
Like memory the blood congeals in it;
And like memory, too, the sun recedes
Into the hazy, southern distances.

A vagrant heat hangs on the dark river,
And shadows turn like smoke. An owl ascends
Among the branches, clattering, remote
Within its motion, intricate with age.

II. The Dream

Mammedaty saw to the building of this house.
Just there, by the arbor, he made a camp in the
old way. And in the evening when the hammers had
fallen silent and there were frogs and crickets
in the black grass—and a low, hectic wind upon
the pale, slanting plane of the moon's light—
he settled deep down in his mind to dream. He
dreamed of dreaming, and of the summer breaking
upon his spirit, as drums break upon the intervals
of the dance, and of the gleaming gourds.

III. The Dance

Dancing,
He dreams, he dreams—
The long wind glances, moves
Forever as a music to the mind;
The gourds are flashes of the sun.
He takes the inward, mincing steps
Describing old processions and refrains.

Dancing,
His moccasins,
His sash and bandolier
Contain him in insignia;
His fan is powerful, concise
According to his agile hand,
And catches on the sacramental air.

IV. The Give-away

Someone spoke his name, Mammedaty, in which
his essence was and is. It was a serious matter
that his name should be spoken there in the circle,
among the many people, and he was thoughtful,
full of wonder, and aware of himself and of his name.
He walked slowly to the summons, looking into the
eyes of the man who summoned him. For a moment
they held each other in close regard, and all about
them there was excitement and suspense.

Then a boy came suddenly into the circle, leading
a black horse. The boy ran, and the horse after him.
He brought the horse up short in front of Mammedaty,
and the horse wheeled and threw its head and cut
its eyes in the wild way. And it blew hard and
quivered in its hide so that light ran, rippling,
upon its shoulders and its flanks—and then it
stood still and was calm. Its mane and tail were
fixed in braids and feathers, and a bright red chief's
blanket was draped in a roll over its withers. The
boy placed the reins in Mammedaty's hands. And all
of this was for Mammedaty, in his honor, as even now
it is in the telling, and will be, as long as there
are those who imagine him in his name.

Earth and I Gave You Turquoise

Earth and I gave you turquoise
   when you walked singing
We lived laughing in my house
   and told old stories
You grew ill when the owl cried
We will meet on Black Mountain

I will bring corn for planting
   and we will make fire
Children will come to your breast
   You will heal my heart
I speak your name many times
The wild cane remembers you

My young brother's house is filled
   I go there to sing
We have not spoken of you
   but our songs are sad
When Moon Woman goes to you
I will follow her white way

Tonight they dance near Chinle
   by seven elms
There you loom whispered beauty
   They will eat mutton
and drink coffee till morning
You and I will not be there

I saw a crow by Red Rock
  standing on one leg
It was the back of your hair
  The years are heavy
I will ride the swiftest horse
You will hear the drumming hooves

The Eagle-Feather Fan

The eagle is my power,
And my fan is an eagle.
It is strong and beautiful
In my hand. And it is real.
My fingers hold upon it
As if the beaded handle
Were the twist of bristlecone.
The bones of my hand are fine
And hollow; the fan bears them.
My hand veers in the thin air
Of the summits. All morning
It scuds on the cold currents;
All afternoon it circles
To the singing, to the drums.

Rainy Mountain Cemetery

Most is your name the name of this dark stone.
Deranged in death, the mind to be inheres
Forever in the nominal unknown,
The wake of nothing audible he hears
Who listens here and now to hear your name.

The early sun, red as a hunter's moon,
Runs in the plain. The mountain burns and shines;
And silence is the long approach of noon
Upon the shadow that your name defines—
And death this cold, black density of stone.

Pit Viper

The cordate head meanders through himself:
Metamorphosis. Slowly the new thing,
Kindled to flares along his length, curves out.
From the evergreen shade where he has lain,
Through inland seas and catacombs he moves.
Blurred eyes that ever see have seen him waste,
Acquire, and undiminished: have seen death—
Or simile—come nigh and overcome.
Alone among his kind, old, almost wise,
Mere hunger cannot urge him from this drowse.

Simile

What did we say to each other
that now we are as the deer
who walk in single file
with heads high
with ears forward
with eyes watchful
with hooves always placed on firm ground
in whose limbs there is latent flight

Trees and Evening Sky

I saw the black trees leaning
In different ways, their limbs
Tangled on the mottled clouds,
The clouds rolling on themselves;
A wide belt of four colors,
Yellow, orange, red, and black;
And stars in the tangled limbs.

Plainview: 3

The sun appearing: a pendant
of clear cutbeads, flashing;
a drift of pollen and glitter
lapping, and overlapping night;
a prairie fire.

The Story of a Well-Made Shield

Now in the dawn before it dies, the eagle swings low
and wide in a great arc, curving downward to the place
of origin. There is no wind, but there is a long roaring
on the air. It is like the wind—nor is it quite like the
wind—but more powerful.

But Then and There the Sun Bore Down

But then and there the sun bore down
And was a focal length away.
The brain was withered and burned brown
And gone to ashes, cold and gray.

Angle of Geese

How shall we adorn
Recognition with our speech?
　Now the dead firstborn
Will lag in the wake of words.

　Custom intervenes;
We are civil, something more:
　More than language means,
The mute presence mulls and marks.

　Almost of a mind,
We take measure of the loss;
　I am slow to find
The mere margin of repose.

　And one November
It was longer in the watch,
　As if forever,
Of the huge ancestral goose.

　So much symmetry!—
Like the pale angle of time
　And eternity.
The great shape labored and fell.

　Quit of hope and hurt,
It held a motionless gaze
　Wide of time, alert,
On the dark distant flurry.

Dana Naone

Dana Naone was born in 1949 in Kaneohe, a windward coast town on the island of Oahu, Hawaii, and has lived there all her life. She is part-Hawaiian and part-English, Chinese and Portuguese.

A 1974 graduate of the University of Hawaii, Naone has taught in the Poets in the Schools Program since its inception in Hawaii three years ago. She is also editor of *Hawaii Review*, which publishes the works of young Hawaiian writers as well as more established national and international artists.

For N. Scott Momaday

For Dana Naone

Girl with the Green Skirt

She walks down the road,
her green skirt floating around her knees.

The men she passes peel off their shirts
and jump into her wide green hem.
She keeps walking, her skirt
clear as the surface of a pond.

Now they hold their arms out from their sides
like the branches of a tree, but no one is fooled
when the birds fly past them and nest
in the green forest of her skirt.

Unaware of the hot wind swirling around
the cool skirt keeps going.
The men following behind are thirsty
for the water of crushed leaves.

Falling into the deep grass
they want to live with green forever.

Long Distance

I had been sitting for days
trying to bite off my right breast
in hope of becoming an Amazon.
You appeared as a repairman
and went straight to the switch-
board behind my stomach.
A strange orange bird had been
pecking through all the wires.
You killed the bird and used
its feathers to make new connections.
My first call was to Egypt.
All the cobras came to the phone
flaring and hissing.

Untitled

I make all the poetic pauses
    outside your door,
paying hurried heed to the stars,
thinking, by now, you must be
    catching my moondrift.
Not seeing you for a few days
has put teeth in my fingertips
    when I touch your legs.
The flute of my desire pipes
a tune upon the fingerholes
    of your imagination.
A great bird rises from your chest
with wings that fill the room.

The Presence

Sometimes I catch a glimpse of it,
a glimmer, like a gold claw
retracting.
In the light that flows around the wood
everything has a life of its own.
The blue shirt draped over the chair
belongs to no one.
It has more than three dimensions,
and changes shape while I watch—
all the time hiding an amused look
in the eyes beneath the collar.

Sleep

Driving late at night I pass
a house with lights still on inside.
It is the body glowing in sleep.
The door opens. Light pours out
like music played in a closed room.
A white figure steps through
and leaps into the dark.

Duane Niatum

Duane Niatum was born in 1938 in Seattle, Washington. A member of the Klallam tribe, he spent his early youth in Washington and California.

After serving in the U.S. Navy, he graduated from the University of Washington and received his M.A. from Johns Hopkins University. He spent two years of his naval service in Japan and feels that his poetry reflects the influence of Oriental culture as well as his interests in painting and music, and, of course, his own Indian heritage.

His poetry has been published in the *Chicago Review*, *Prairie Schooner*, *Northwest Review* and numerous other literary journals. He has also published two books of poems, *After the Death of an Elder Klallam* (Baleen Press) and *Ascending Red Cedar Moon* (Harper & Row).

Chief Leschi of the Nisqually

He awoke this morning from a strange dream—
Thunderbird wept for him in the blizzard.
Holding him in their circle, Nisqually women
Turn to the river, dance to its song.

He burned in the forest like a red cedar,
His arms fanning blue flames toward
The white men claiming the *camas* valley
For their pigs and fowl.
Musing over wolf tracks vanishing in snow,
The memory of his wives and children
Keeps him mute. Flickering in the dawn fires,
His faith grows roots, tricks the soldiers
Like a fawn, sleeping black as the brush.

They laugh at his fate, frozen as a bat
Against his throat. Still, death will take
Him only to his father's longhouse,
Past the flaming rainbow door. These bars
Hold but his tired body; he will eat little
And speak less before he hangs.

Ascending Red Cedar Moon

for Philip and Ann McCracken

I

Out of friendship and a slow retreat of the blood,
I stop to watch Sun give away
Its morning names, among petroglyphs
Of spear, trap, and drum.
Streaming ocher threads over the salmon ceremony,
Rain falls in four directions.
And wind hails grandfather at *N'huia-wulsh,*
After greeting the village moss, shells,
Berry and water baskets. Children
Circle the Elders in half the moon who carve
Their lives into this totemic dream.

My son has run off somewhere,
Perhaps to discover the thundering hawk,
The rainbow beauty of deer
Turning like sunlit streaks down the path.
Or maybe he is learning how to fall,
Make room for pain and the nightmare in his heart,
Rest with bear in the ear of the blizzard?
Like Niatum, his great-great grandfather,
He believes in bluejay's humor,
The legends in the long dives of killer whale,
Will lead him to fern-shadowed meadows,
The Elwah river's thousand-year elegy to Spring.
With the gift of the blind,
He may turn these roots into song or to dance.

My sweet woman, keeper of the poem,
Floats like a waterbug,
A naked fan of sunlight.
I will lie with her soon in the soft,
Secret room of willows.

II

In Owl's light, we held hands with the fire
And the moon spreading its feathers
Over the *Ho-had-hun* sky.
Now dancing in honor of the Seven Brothers,
The drums grow quiet as the river birds,
And we see First People step
From the graves of rotting white fir.
The Elders rise first in greeting;
It has been so long since the Klallams
Have heard such a weeping:

> *Chee chako.*   *An-na-du!*   *An-na-du!*
> *Mox-pooh.*   *Mox-pooh.*

Indian Rock, Bainbridge Island, Washington

for Mary Randlett

When you reach to touch the markings
On my face, step from the lodge
Of patience, then listen to the order
Of sand and cedar, totem and fishnet,
Blossom and oyster,
Gulls diving into surfaces,
Green journeys of salmon,
Time sapping the season
Of the red-breasted woodpecker.

When you are as motionless as the crane
In the cattails, breathing like the tide,
Then I will chant the legend
To help you hear the paddles thrust,
The rattling bones, the chattering masks,
Your dead ancestors dancing down the beach.

When the long-leaf rains have chilled
Your bones in the morning gale,
Changed your direction to the cottage,
Your drive to the city,
I will end the whaler's song,
Leaving you alone to bend like the reed.

Elegy for Chief Sealth (1786–1866)

The white man will never be alone.
Let him be just and deal kindly with my people,
For the dead are not powerless.

Compromised by sorrow,
You stand at the rim of the diminishing forest,
Your face leathered by salt winds
From the Sound inlets,
The sacred *camas* islands of your fathers,
And chant for your eightieth moon going blind.

Because the Guardian Spirits
Coot like pipers of the white man's flood
From the Eastern seaboard,
You hear death calling you to burn alone
In the fire of the black sun.
The waves of ships, covered wagons,
Broke your arrows, pierced your shield,
Silenced the eagle in your heart, long-paralyzed
By their eyes screaming Alaska gold.

Yet, as if a drumbeat
From the first *Duwamish* dancers, your remaining
Tribes slowly regain a part of their soil,
Turning your people's grief to a small joy,
Like sighting the dreaming crane,
The reed's lost shadow.

On Hearing the Marsh Bird's Water Cry

for William Stafford

I

I stand within the willowing shadows of *Memp-ch-ton*,
Digging for arrowhead and rattle
My ancestors pared from earth and rotting pines.
N'huia-wulsh, their abandoned village,
Lives in the wolfprint's eye,
Emerges with the whale at the peak of sunset,
Rings like peace markings undulating past
The white fir clearings. There are many ways
To listen to the bones: to start is to strip naked,
Bend to face the moon in the Elwah river.

II

My mind now on its own journey moves like coyote
Over the camp's black mirror.
The first layer speaks of a long dive under water,
The second count the salmon's heartbeat as your symbol,
The third swim deep and bleed like a shark.

III

The Elders managed the invasion by living in the foliage
Of their Thunderbird, dancing until they dropped.
I watch Chief Joseph, Leschi, and Sealth
Retire into the forest's secret longhouse,
Without desire for suicide or defeat;
These men teach me how to eat mushrooms and grow silent.
I dance with Death until our breath is stone.
First Salmon flashes in his eyes,
Balancing faith in the marsh of the loon's cry.

 Carriers of the Dream Wheel 122

IV

The last summit lays a full basket on the ground:
Never knife the hermit in your soul,
Stand still in this stone blade in the red cedar moon,
Listen to the shamans roam through stars.

No One Remembers Abandoning the Village of White Fir

I

As a child of cedar, hemlock, and the sea,
I often slept under totem and star,
Sometimes hanging under the black lids
Of a bat's closed eyes to seal off
My soul from the drone of my mother's wrath.

Time formed itself from rimes of the Elwah,
Rainbow river of my ancestors,
Whose arts were fishing, hunting,
Dance, and occasionally war.
Winds then clacked like bone rattles,
Shaking lost meters from the dark.
Many salmon still swim the rapid dreams
Of those children left alone with bluejay and chipmunk.
And when the shaman called to wolf,
I sealed up cave after cave.

II

Dancing back to eagle's nest, our blood sang.
Soon hearing river's morning song,
I followed its shadow into the sky,
Reached the snowy tip of *Memp-ch-ton*'s white wing.
At the summit, wild rose and lupine
Hid like worms from the stone's avalanche.

On other days, I ran through a childhood
Of a dozen myths, seeing the fruit on the tree
In the light of Black Cherries Moon
As memories to be plucked for my escape
From the wreckage of scars.

III

Crawling into the cave of another nightmare,
I was left furless, a bear, clawing
Its way past the hissing, howling blizzard.
Seatco chased me to the edge of my cries.
Coyote tossed me into death's arms.
An old man who appeared in the blackwinged passage,
Sadly shook his head,
Shamed by my fear, but not my failure.
Grandfather, you and Great Uncle
Were the only men I have known:
Your spirits have been my shield;
Someday, may I step in the shadow of your courage,
Offer your songs to the children and nameless poor?

IV

Figures on the outer sides of baskets
Move quietly through morning;
The women are first to see the sun reach the river.
Hoping to live through the vision,
An Elder awakens to the wrens,
Tosses the moon out for one more night.

V

Spinning on colors of the unfinished meadow,
The earth covers up her past
With a celebration of wind and acorn;
Hears women and children picking
Roots and laughing. Today, these paths disappear
Like hawk, deer, the fern dreamers.
And this eroding wood barely draws the stranger
Into the clearing, the red-bone center of sunrise.

VI

Watching for the shifts in the yellow leaf fire,
I seek the glow of a cedar cone in ash,
An offering to burn in the city,
Until I see the face of *O-le-man* smile
Before vanishing in the rainbow,
Motioning me to return to wolf's chant
Round the fire that starts the morning song.

Never quite as constant as the moon,
I speak to the bats once again—
Stop when Trickster calls

    "Niatum! Niatum!"

Old Woman Awaiting the Greyhound Bus

Almost singing, she stares past the crowd and flies.
Wearing a black-knit shawl that has fed
Generations of moths, warmed the small bodies
Of many grandchildren, her face wrinkles
Into a smiling heap of eggshells.
Seeing me watching her, she asks me to sit down,
Her baroque cane pinning her age to the floor
Like an icon. I see those grandchildren
In her eyes do figure eights on thin ice,
Flooding her dreaming with their forgotten jokes.

Her smile then fades to an apple left to brown
On a bedroom table four generations asleep,
And in blue humility, free of remembrances,
She drops her teeth into the grave of appearances
At the bottom of her purse, now
Somewhere in a room of yellow voices.

No longer caring about the odds in her age,
Her mind breathes with the apple peasants of the world,
And chews time like a white rabbit.

On Leaving Baltimore

I

Memory pales in the face of the moon,
Shedding it like a skin.
Silence opens the window, the door, the mirror.
Condemning all to the teeth,
It steps into the street everyone's heard tear
Owl from the oak, scanning the field.

II

A falling star heaves the word against the wall.
Dodging this way, then that, I hope
The wind stays lost in history.
That damn owl. For years I've been waiting
For it to speak up, announce the dream is a fraud,
Send the insomniac back to the bed
That haunts him like a bat.

III

A weary stone drags its way toward the river.
Wanting to say I understand,
Ask if it needs a hand, but before I can speak,
Owl swoops down, drowning my voice.

IV

If a god is around, he, she, or it must wonder
What link snapped when death suddenly gasped,
Choked, then kept on chanting. Now the only fugitives
That see hope alone are the alders,
Happy as winds put storm away to sleep.
Their roots burrow like moles beneath the swamp.

V

Parading along the crevice of my eye, forever
Doing its eight-legged dance,
Spider starts the long trek through the doors,
The windows, the mirror, off to the hills, mud.
Exhausted, everyone watches for time
To shake like a skeleton. Even the mountains
Hail the avalanche of sand and sea,
Bursting from the rip in the sun.

On Visiting My Son, Port Angeles, Washington

I

Tides shape the sides of the agate mountain,
Drifting wood, man, and animal,
Alerting the town to the talking dreams
Of strangers. Marc lives with his mother here,
Almost steps like cougar in high country,
Proud, silent, ready to roam by himself.
Growing quickly to the songs and sorrows
Of fisherman and shaman, he's now
Crane leaning toward the age of full leaf moon.

II

We wander the waterfront pier by pier,
November air bringing pure
Oxygen to our lungs. Listening to ducks,
We ride in the ships gliding seaward
In the snow-deep sun.
Settled in the wave's return,
My son drifts in the rhythm of the sea,
Slowing my heart to a piper's cry.
I am filled with joy
To see he has no more need of me
Than a hawk needs the sun.
His concentration leaves me short of breath—
His face staring into the singing mirror,
Reflects the breaker's white wingtips.

III

In this pacific, my Grandfather joined
Us for a moment, appearing as a water guardian.
This cedar man offers my son a century
Of legend to season in, then retreats
After our walk has ended. Like First Father,
He points to Marc laughing
At the mud hens, surfacing from underneath the pier.

The Novelty Shop

More grotesque than a row of laundromats,
A haze of pawnshops,
Novel shopkeepers pun Seattle
Like skid row. Outside the entrance
A cigar-store Indian, with the entombed
Stare of a museum sculpture,
Draws the tourists from the East
Into the damp shop of seashore ornaments
For manufactured bores. With the forest
Serenity of a shaman, the black eyes
Of a shaker, Eagle Runner
Abandons the city of red rain, and dives
Into the sea at the end of the pier.

Crow's Way

Myth lilies. A smog-edge sky blurs his eyes
Like a cataract. The pond is abstract, a green
Ripple flowing through the frog, discovering
Wind has no direction, no word on summer.
He won't laugh at frog, if it won't laugh at him;
He's come to purge the fly-swarmed loneliness.
At thirty-three, it's neither self-indulgence,
Nor a loser's plea to wear a freedom mask.
Now he's maskless as the birch and half as white.
And glacier sun leaves him naked to the bone:
For cedar child lies grounded, opaque, invisible
As the traveler. So he wonders if he was
This boy who swam in *Hoko* river light
To help moon find her feathers in the snowy pools.

To Your Question

I

The day you appeared I began to speak
More gently to the woman lying in my field.
Your smile penetrated my nightmare
Like the faint cry of a sparrow.
You turned, your eyes were warm as feathers.
Again, I was shamed by my bitterness, exile.

II

I write this brief poem because your world
Is your family's and is new to me,
And to tell you poets sing to themselves
What they long to write to you.
The wind measures the counterpoint to frost,
Scattering maple leaves like a fugue.

III

The shimmering image of your body lingers
As shadows from the lake, breaking
In the dawn fiction. I touch from memory
Your delicate thin hands, holding
Them like a gift from the blind.
I am trying to understand your fear that we
Might be singing for two different moons.

After the third time around, I step toward
The street and home, wondering if the lake's
Green mirror and the morning will cross
The landscape of your question, open your blossom
To the sun, blazing in the cattails.

Homage to Chagall

I

The candle takes the first desperate
Leap through the window, flaming a rainbow
To the black valley on the moon.

In a corner, a weary juggler feeds his heart
This star; then decides to tumble
Inside the blue cow's crystal ball,

Seven songs, circling night and day.
He is joyous, and no one thinks this strange;
Besides, the town has stopped the rage

For burying their lies in the goat's footprints.
Quite happy for a moment, the synagogue
Crier trades songs for spring rain.

Sleepy children on their way to school
Watch the bearded violinist strand music
On the poplar trees; laughing, the green rabbi

Puns the Czar in Hebrew: for decades, police
Have rolled off the ghetto wall like dice.

II

And his love for woman is a peacock's dance
At sunset. Like Redon, Monet, Picasso,
He masters her lean curves along the body

Of the dream, where Eros hails painter and magician.
After catching the blossom from the "Sun at Poros,"
Our bodies turn into reeds, our eyes into nomads.

Slow Dancer That No One Hears but You

(after an intaglio by Kevin Cuddy)

She, the sensual creature, the green singer,
Interpreter of the moon's stone calendar,
Sweet fragrant wanderer through your forest,
Calls you with the ambivalence of the wind.
When she walks with you, the calligraphy
Of maple leaves reveal our lost histories:
The soul's abstract vagabonds.

The way her song paints the owl's white face
On the black mask of the pine hillside
Suggests her desire may be to reach the heart
From memory, trembling in its nakedness,
A bold flame dancing in the moonlit clearing.
Is not her lover one of the thin Tricksters
Moving closer? Inside, far from the sleeping

Crowd, her stare marks a serene eye of departure.
How she arrived at the beginning of sleep
Drives you on and on through the fields,
Running from shadow to shadow, toward her hand
That is never quite within reach,
But somehow encouraging, so you go on, knowing
She is what is real, important for your death.

Forever smiling, her green pupils radiate your
Hard desire, and she starts to set you free,
Brush her fingers across your soul's icon.
From now on, falling to sleep will be easier—
She has left her blue dancers in the wind,
River echoes of the women who fled.

After the Death of an Elder Klallam

I

You sat with a bottle of beer
In one hand, and a steaming mussel in the other,
Chanting in The Moon of Dry Grass,
The story of *Kwatee*, the Changer.
Your grandchildren huddled,
Awed by your heavy-lumbered frame
And demonic shadow painted in the sand by fire.
When your laughter cracked in pine
Logs that smelled of kelp and seaweed,
We saw the totem surface with killer whale.

Twelve salmon harvests have passed
Since I last saw your fishnets
Hanging through winter across the common stream.
What blizzard afternoon was it
When you pantomimed the legend of black elk
Who was only seen by Trickster;
And the Chinook salmon held in a net,
And because of his copper eyes and flapping
Defiance, you threw him to the sea?
And when did the taste for the whale hunt
Darken to nothing more than myth?

One morning you fed feast bones
To Herring People, we heard you shouting
Obscenities at the crows,
After slipping on a heap of crab shells.

II

Today, nettles and serviceberry hide
Your home, and the stone animals
You carved before the entrance to your longhouse
Mirror rainbows of your children's children.
What are blue forests without you, Granduncle?
Who else but your brother or sister
Sees the forest breathing when woodpecker
Is silent? How long before the village
Vanished like ashes did you begin to die?
Was it on the reservation you kept running from?
At your son's death, or your brother's?
Now your children lie stripped
Down to their hides, charred saplings of cedar,
Old roots in soil of many seasons.

III

In the winds of Thunderbird, I chant
To Mount *Memp-ch-ton*, under the yew tree shield,
As Great Uncle did before the sea
Called him back to live with oyster and sand,
Soothe the hunger of crab and fish.

Seeing him wave to us in the amber silence,
We watch for salmon to fin dark
Rapids of sapphire to the spawning beds
in *Ho-had-hun* creeks.

At the *N'huia-wulsh* ruins, the white fir
Village of his blood, Old Man
Drums to green moon's rising, in memory
Of his brothers, the lost fishermen and singers,
Then closes his eyes to follow
The glacier's light to the cave.

IV

As brother to chickadee and wolf,
Rain soaked and restless,
I reach my heart in the earth of these cedarmen,
In the dream songs of my Great Uncle,
Joseph, elder to hawk and sparrow.

For Duane Niatum

For Simon J. Ortiz

Simon J. Ortiz

Simon J. Ortiz, an Acoma, was born in Albuquerque, New Mexico, in 1941. He served three years in the Army and then attended the Universities of New Mexico and Iowa, the latter as a Fellow in the International Writing Program. He has taught at San Diego State University, the Institute of American Indian Arts, and Navajo Community College. His poetry has previously been published in various anthologies and journals, including the *New Mexico Quarterly*.
Ortiz is currently living in Albuquerque, New Mexico. He has a wife, Naomi, and two children, Raho Nez and Rainy Dawn.

To Insure Survival

for my daughter Rainy Dawn, born on July 5, 1973

You come forth
the color of a stone cliff
at dawn,
changing colors,
blue to red,
to all the colors of the earth.

Grandmother Spider speaks
laughter and growing
and weaving things
and threading them
together to make life
to wear;
all these, all these.

You come out, child,
naked as that cliff at sunrise,
shorn of anything
except spots of your mother's blood.
You just kept blinking your eyes
and trying to catch your breath.

In five more days,
they will come,
singing, dancing,
bringing gifts,
the stones with voices,
the plants with bells.
They will come.

Child, they will come.

The Creation: According to Coyote

"First of all, it's all true."
Coyote, he says this, this way,
humble yourself, motioning and meaning
what he says.

You were born when you came
from that body, the earth;
your black head burst from granite,
the ashes cooling

until it began to rain.
It turned muddy then,
and then green and brown things
came without legs.

They looked strange.
Everything was strange.
There was nothing to know then,

until later, Coyote told me this,
and he was bullshitting probably,
two sons were born,
Uyuyayeh and Masawe.

They were young then
and then later on they were older.

And then the people were wondering
what was above.
They had heard rumors.

But, you know, Coyote,
he was mainly bragging
when he said (I think),
"My brothers, the Twins then said,
'Let's lead these poor creatures
and save them.' "

And later on, they came to light
after many exciting
and colorful and tragic things
having to do with adventure,
and this is the life, all these, all these.

My uncle told me all this, that time.
Coyote told me too, but you know
how he is, always talking to the gods,
and mountains, the stone all around

And you know, I believe him.

A San Diego Poem:
January–February 1973

The Journey Begins

My son tells his aunt,
"You take a feather,
and you have white stuff in your hand,
and you go outside,
and you let the white stuff fall to the ground.
That's praising."

In the morning, take cornfood outside,
say words within and without.
Being careful, breathe in and out,
praying for sustenance, for strength,
and to continue safely and humbly,
you pray.

Shuddering

The plane lifts off the ground.
The shudder of breaking from earth
gives me a splitsecond of emptiness.
From the air, I can only give substance
and form to places I am familiar with.
I only see shadows and darkness
of mountains and the colored earth.

The jet drones heavily.
Stewardesses move along the aisles.
Passengers' faces are normally bland,
and oftentimes I have yearned, achingly,
for a sharp, distinctive face, someone

who has a stark history, even a killer
or a tortured saint, but most times
there is only the blandness.

I seek association with earth.
I feel trapped, fearful of enclosures.
I wait for the Fasten Seat Belt sign
to go off, but when it does
I don't unfasten my belt.

The earth is red in eastern Arizona,
mesa cliffs, the Chinle formation
is an ancient undersea ridge lasting
for millions of years.
I find the shape of whale still lingers.
I see it flick gracefully by Sonsela Butte
heading for the Grand Canyon.

I recite the cardinal points of my Acoma life,
the mountains, the radiance coming
from those sacred points, gathering
into the center.
What is it, the movement of this journey,
in this jet above the earth?
I wonder about that.

Coming into L.A. International Airport,
I look below at the countless houses,
row after row, veiled by tinted smog.
I feel the beginnings of apprehension.
Where am I? I recall the institutional prayers
of my Catholic youth but don't dare recite them.
The prayers of my native selfhood
have been strangled in my throat.

The Fasten Seat Belt sign has come back on
and the jet drone is more apparent in my ears.
I picture the moments in my life
when I have been close enough to danger
to feel the vacuum prior to death
when everything stalls.
The shudder of returning to earth
is much like breaking away from it.

Under L.A. International Airport

Numbed by the anesthesia of jet flight,
I stumble into the innards of L.A. International.
Knowing that they could not comprehend,
I dare not ask questions of anyone.
I sneak furtive glances at TV schedule consoles
and feel their complete ignorance of my presence.
I allow an escalator to carry me downward;
it deposits me before a choice of tunnels.
Even with a clear head, I've never been good
at finding my way out of American labyrinths.
They all look alike to me. I search
for a distinct place, a familiar plateau,
but in the tunnel, on the narrow alley's wall,
I can only find bleak small-lettered signs.
At the end of that tunnel, I turn a corner
into another and get the unwanted feeling
that I am lost. My apprehension is unjustified
because I know where I am I think.
I am under L.A. International Airport,
on the West Coast, someplace called America.
I am somewhat educated, I can read and use a compass;
yet the knowledge of where I am is useless.
Instead it is a sad, disheartening burden.
I am a poor, tired wretch in this maze.

With its tunnels, its jet drones, its bland faces,
TV consoles, and its emotionless answers,
America has obliterated my sense of comprehension
Without this comprehension, I am emptied
of any substance. America has finally caught me.
I melt into the walls of that tunnel
and become the silent burial. There are no echoes.

A Pretty Woman

We came to the edge
of the mesa
and looked below.

We could see
the shallow wash
snaking down
from the cut
between two mesas,
all the way from Black Mountain;

and the cottonwoods
from that distance
looked like a string of turquoise,

and the land was a pretty woman
smiling at us
looking at her.

What I Tell Him

I take my son outside
and show him a tree,
have him touch leaves,
this is a leaf, see,
it is green, it's got lines,
and it is shaped this way,
touch.
He touches the leaf
and branch trembles with his touch,
fat little hands roughly
and gently grasping what I show him.
Make him stand, bare feet,
on the ground, feel
that dirt, brown dirt and gravel,
solid clay, it won't grow seed
too well, have to have sand,
and leaves, sticks, manure,
and then it will grow things.
That's what I tell him.

Waiting for You to Come By

all those summers, waiting,
hot, tensing with sounds that don't come,
the wind puts circles
            in which your mind is enclosed
waiting
for thoughts to follow,
anywhere, just so the thoughts
come.
          they don't come,
just the hot wind, dancing steady, deadening
the moments not paying attention to history,
the flesh without motion, waiting
         for the sound without motion.

come here girl. come here. come.
i have been waiting
so long. these days are impossible,
blessings so vague that they are not even dreams,
i can't see the stars on the horizon,
time has stopped. time has stopped.

i have been waiting
for you to come by.

Forming Child Poems

First One

O child's tremble
against your mother's innerwall,
is a true movement
without waste or hesitation,
a beating of wings
following ancient trails
to help us return.

Second One

I will point
out your place on the earth,
among mountains, on ground,
by old watercourses, in wind,
where your mother walked,
where her mother walked.
This way then,
this way,
I will show you those points
where you will present yourself.

Third One

Two days ago
when I was at the foot
of Black Mountain,
there were rain clouds forming
in a space
between the tip of the mountain
and a point in the sky.
Two days before that,

I saw a hawk circling
in a slow, cool wind
south of that place
where I stood watching.

Fourth One

Years ago, your brother and I
walked from Chee Goodluck's hogan
in the Lukachukai mountains
to a place where water flowed
from under huge granite boulders.
The water tasted like the wind,
roots, fresh herbs, sweet smells.

Fifth One

I want you to see a pass
in the Chuska mountains
where there is aspen, oak,
elevation high enough
for fir and snow
enough to last until June.
I've been up there twice,
once on a hard winter day.

Sixth One

Among the things I would require
of you, is that you should relish
the good wheat bread your mother makes,
taking care that you should think
how her hands move, kneading the dough,
shaping it with her concern,
and how you were formed and grew in her.

Seventh One

Near the summit, SE of Kinlichee,
I saw a piece of snowmelt water
that I thought would look good
on a silver bracelet with maybe
two small stones of turquoise at its sides;
but then, I liked the way it was, too,
under some pine trees, the snow feeding it,
and the evening sun slanting off it,
and knew that you would understand
why I decided to leave it like that.

Eighth One

Yesterday, as I was lighting a cigarette,
Raho warned me with,
"If anyone starts a fire,
Smokey the Bear will come put them out."
Bear's got a lot of friends.

The Serenity in Stones

I am holding this turquoise
in my hands.
My hands hold the sky
wrought in this little stone.
There is a cloud
at the furthest boundary.
The world is somewhere underneath.

I turn the stone, and there is more sky.
This is the serenity possible in stones,
the place of a feeling to which one belongs.
I am happy as I hold this sky
in my hands, in my eyes, and in myself.

Watching Salmon Jump

for Angelina,
whom I knew in my youthful hunger
as Frances

It was you:
I could have crawled
between mountains—
that is where seeds are possible—
and touched the soft significance
of roots
of birth and the smell of newborn fish
                    and
know how it is
leaping into rock
so that my children may survive

Bony

My father brought that dog home
in a gunny sack.

The reason we called it Bony
was because it was skin and bones.

It was a congenital problem
or something that went way back
into its dog's history.

We loved it without question,
its history and ours.

Survival This Way

Survival, I know how this way.
This way, I know.
It rains.
Mountains and canyons and plants
grow.
We travelled this way,
gauged our distance by stories
and loved our children.
We taught them
to love their births.
We told ourselves over and over
again, "We shall survive
this way."

Anita Endrezze Probst

Anita Endrezze Probst was born in 1952 in Long Beach, California. She is half Yaqui Indian and a mixture of Austrian, Italian, Swiss, Hungarian, Spanish and German. She has lived in California, Hawaii and Washington.

A 1973 honors graduate of Eastern Washington State College, she also received an M.A. in creative writing from that school. She is currently living in Spokane where she teaches in an alternate education program for drop-outs and minority students of high school age.

Her poems have appeared in numerous magazines, including the *Malahat Review*, the *Blue Cloud Quarterly*, the *Dacotah Territory*, and *Indian Voice*.

Manifest Destiny

Feathers blacken against the sun
rising like the songs of old warriors,
past whitened skies to die.
I tried too hard to stop the cold wind
from blowing across the miles of my cheeks
so death brought summer, fever bright.
Oh, Indian woman, you carried your corn
in small red pots with painted turquoise
rivers, and now the pots are broken
like your ancient bones. With no wings
to flee from me, my memory dreams your spirit face
and I see you sleeping in shallow blue shade.
My mother used to say, Brown Child
of the red sand, wash your feet
with river flowers, climb high
upon the rocks and smile out
the stars. Now as a woman,
I remember a man who said
all Indians are rich
they just don't know how to save,
except by cans of beer.
And like the buffalo, you took my brown
skin and hung it on the wall.
I am gentle, but angry:
Is this how you white men
mount your trophies. Tomorrow, I see
my son; in his eyes there is more than quiet pain—
now blood-red flames bloom anger
and he has yet to live.

Red Rock Ceremonies

The clear moon arcs
over the sleeping Three Sisters,
like the conchos that string
the waist of a dancer.

With low thunder, with red bushes smooth
as water stones, with the blue-arrowed rain,
its dark feathers curving down
and the white-tailed running deer—
the desert sits, a maiden with obsidian eyes,
brushing the star-tasseled dawn from her lap.

It is the month of Green Corn;
It is the dance, grandfather, of open blankets.

  I am singing to you
  I am making the words
   shake like bells.

Owl Woman is blessing all directions.
This corn—with its leaves that are yellow
in the sun, with the green of small snakes,
with its Mother Earth's hair and even teeth,
with its long leaves, its dark stem,
and the small blue bird that drinks from its roots—
you are shaking purple in dusk,
you are climbing the rims of the world.

Old grandfather, we are combing your hair
for blue stars and black moons.
With white corn, with cloud feathers,
you are crossing dawn without the Dream Runners.

I am closing your blanket
I am making the words
        speak in circles.

The Truth about My Sister and Me

When I was a child
I never smiled;
the faces of people
scared me too much.

She liked to wear her jeans rolled twice
with dirt and rocks caught in between
and her yellowed socks turned inside out;
she liked not taking baths and being mean,
drinking kool-aid like whiskey
in plastic glasses that bounced
when dropped from behind a third-story screen.

When I was a child
I never was a child;
I knew I grew myself
and the sky came down to me.

She owned the sidewalk freeways;
collecting pennies from others who dared
the dangerous block of skateboards
and tricycles; stop lights glared
from flannel topped cans
that rang-jangled with coins
and marbles carefully paired.

When I was that young
how gracefully I sung
"Silent Night" alone in the snow,
mocking those who stood at doors.

She is older, lean, running with ease:
her legs stopping the cars at the light,
capturing the baker and both of his sons,
licking jelly from her fingers each night;
her smooth thighs pumping for a goal
of ice-whiskey dresses and new dollar bills,
rolled, like her smile, into pockets too tight.

When I was a child
and loving wild,
I never saw a woman die
from living.

The Stripper

I

On the stage, mirrored many times,
my body is cubed and squared,
sequined and feathered, bare
and rounded, bright and hot
under the lights and sweaty stares;
drum roll, grinding hips, pivot
swing, cupping my warm hands slowly
up to my breast, slipping off
the red laced bra in twenty wet sighs
unfastening silk underwear to reveal
skin dark fur, musty stroke of things,
while they grasp their brown bottles
and I groan, opening my mouth,
looking not at the men below
but at the luminous green exit sign.

II

During the intermissions, I walk over
the thrown coins on the floor, mostly dimes,
into the bathroom to replace
my breasts, flick ashes into toilet bowls
put back my underwear Newberry pink
and fluff out the black feathers:
I always lose some every time.
These lights show the bones carving
through the finish of my face:
Jukebox songs knife years across my lips,
echoing in the hollows of my cheeks,
rattling my tongue dry,
but the only music in here
is the gargle of the toilets
and the sound of its blue beat
matching the wine in my veins.

Learning the Spells: A Diptych

I

The Sorceress Divides the Night

Crush the manroot, swallow what you desire.
Turn twice and put your hands deep in flames.
Your fingers will flower violets in black skies,
will curl their soft moons like bright water on fur.

I am the jaguar of his blood,
the dark keeper of his crouching spear;
I learn Night's spells in the body's dreams,
in the eager tight hugging of spittle to mud.

Repeat the cries of pale wolves,
the beginnings and endings of torn flesh;
follow its blood to the river's edge.
Drink in silence; look for the man.
Between the spaces of trees and rushing fire's wings,
he is formed, rising like fog, like fire,
out of the loins of sky and earth
and all that causes limbs to tremble.

Our whispers are pale scorpions;
we fill our hands with stones
small as the eyes of frogs.
We sleep in the stomachs of lions.

II

The Hunter, Bewitched

The nighthawk screams its white trail,
fields rustle like black weasels.
The swelling mounds of grass
grow thickest in the furrowed crotch.
Her breast is rising rock,
sheathed in white moss.
The curving horseshoe moon
is the soft slip of shoulder.

I wake in this blackness called Night.
I know this urge to breathe is Life;
this earth body's heaving grapple of bones and flesh.
Breaking away from soiled womb, I writhe.
I know the Maker of my smallest hair.
I feel the Presence press.

I cannot find her eyes.
Pine cone seeds shake in the wind like dried teeth.
I seek her name in River's heavy blue hair.

I am the beast she never knew or wished. I grieve
with lust: I will split her like the water's reeds.
That damp-backed woman's spell runs, wounded.
It hides, a coiled snake, under silken leaves.
Betrayal flies quietly on dark wings.

Her nails flint a red-starred sky.
Her skin is rain on wet clay.
I root into that dark earth
like the snout of a white-eyed pig.

Notes from an Analyst's Couch

I

I nail Picasso's girl with a mirror
to the back of my head.
I'm giving her reason to live.

Thigh deep in pasture, she is smearing
my father with blood and sweet heavy clover.
She contemplates under the slow mercy
of fading moons. Silver ash seedlings cover her feet.
Her arms, outstreched, point nowhere, east and west.
In silence, I am smothering her with morning glories.
Rootless, they wither to riddles.

A woman sits with sleeping hands,
a gypsy counting my dreams, palming my fate:
my hands are wild horses, rushing away;
she guides the reins, my hooves strike flames,
burning crescents into oceans, spray
catches in her throat like curving swords.
I am seeking a quiet murder.

II

I am saying what I mean to please you.
This couch is too short, my legs are fraying
at the ends, arms snaking up the walls,
gliding behind you to twist your stiff neck.
I will strangle you with these lines.
They are merging, snarling, choking my veins,
reaching out to grab your smoking pencil.
The gypsy is eating lead, shining shoes.
The girl has broken her mirror, my father lives,
all directions point inward. Picasso is dead.
Make the connection, bring us all together.
Tie your notes into one smooth ribbon
and let me hang.

Exodus

To be ten and skinny
is not so bad if you dream,
stone skipping across
the bony parts of your being,
a worm ready to change
unaware of the gnawing outside,
the white fibered veil
destroyed.

You dream of soft sheets
and bells, lace, love, printed cards
with two envelopes, both white
and that strong gentle man
who asks you every time
and listens to your answer.
You dream, dream, and blow bubbles
from your mouth carefully.

Always crossing your legs
and pulling down your skirts,
you never were quite ready
to be dragged across the bricks
by five strange men, who only laughed
and spread your legs
like dried wishbones,
picking away at your red flesh.

Now, when people ask your age
you can not imagine what they mean
and the phone keeps singing in the night,
siren of your childhood;
red lights stream hotly past
the thin fingers lacing your eyes,
brushing away threads of an unwound cocoon;
like your dreams,
it never was quite there.

Canto Llano

All the sisters of mercy
have joined their flat hands,
piercing their palms with roses;
blood ribbons a garland
las flores del psalmos,
las monjas han llorado pérdón.

Las diosas del fuego, me devoré:
como las caras de los santos.

They are a white-hooded cover
of falcons crying;
the slow spread of lilies
growing deep under graves.
Too many hail marys
rot bones as they save.

They are circling
burning round
thick in chants at Yucatan.

Creo ver a Dios
en la locura de sus ojos;
las lunas rojas
las lunas llenas
misa rezada
de trébol blanca.

Their ankles taste bitter
burning round
eyes of dark waters.

Mis hermanas de Sangre Diosas
canto a sus hijas brujas.

All the sisters of mercy
are pregnant with moons.
They circle me,
fingers smoking like candles;
they roll their own stones.
I am on my knees.

Eclipse

I

Squinting against neon signs
and black dressed women,
you've sold your vision for green lightning.
A wild horse with red breath
hides deep within your belly.

You're dying in alleyways
and hot thick bars.
Slipping in foam and vomit,
you warhoop across streets
like a horse on locoweed
or an old man with no eyes.

A star spirit dances with blue heels,
shaking his prayer stick,
calling your name.
It is hidden under every worn stone.

II

Black Wolf, naked night-hunter,
you crouch in the corner and growl.
Your howling eclipses my pleas
and the broken bottles rip open your mouth
with the quick surge of an eagle's anger.

You dark man, trying to hide the blood
and spitting it at me in rage;
baring your raw lips and black tongue,
on all fours you crawl from my lodge
and try to find the moon.
Once you said it was in my eyes.

In the Flight of the Blue Heron:
To Montezuma

The weeping spreads,
In Tlatelolco the tears are dripping.
. . . Yes, already the city of Mexico is abandoned;
the smoke rises; the haze spreads.

—Aztec verse

I

I weave the night, I cross the weft with stars
and the dark hollows of your eyes;
I plait the words you've said into my hair.

II

We held the moon between us,
we carried the sun on our backs
and tied the reeds into boats.
We burned the cities and forgot them.
In the flight of the blue heron,
we left you behind
and *Tamoanchan* starved
like a child.

III

The reeds bend and straighten.
You encircled my arms in bracelets of jade
and crushed the sweet-water rushes
against my thighs. The sun in your eyes
burned the land to white bones and dried
the women in labor. You promised me gold
and silver fluted songs, but when the sea-crossed
warriors came, you sent me away and died.
The birds circled your grave.

The sands move five feet a night,
sifting through my hands,
a showering mountain,
a temple ground yellow-white,
shifting swamps to deserts.

The loom catches my fingers,
carding them of flesh,
whittling the bones into sand;
spinning my voice across the strata
of time. I bend against the wind,
the hissing snake who bids me kiss the sand;
and twist my fingers among the threads,
weaving, weaving.

IV

Do not look at me. I have kept my promise.
I sing to the coyote and turn from the eagle.
I no longer dance. I burrow into the sand,
listening, listening
to the soft drum of sheared hearts,
still glistening in bowls of stone.
The capes of plumed feathers do not fly;
the altars of stone do not give beneath the bodies,
stretched out like wool drying in the sun.

To weave a god, to unravel a life,
I spin and watch the altars
soften to sand against the skins.

V

The sane, swirling through the spindle,
touches and defines your body.
You stare past the dunes, past my face;
that we were lovers once does not stop your death,
does not prevent mine.
The weaving captures colors; the sand blasts them out
and covers the moon, destroys the sun.

My blanket is patterned with signs
the fringes still tied to the frame;
the loom stands like a skeleton
across the Aztec sky.

W. M. Ransom

W. M. Ransom, who is part Cheyenne and Arapaho, was born in Puyallup, Washington, in 1945. He attended Washington State University and the University of Puget Sound on athletic scholarships and received his B.A. from the University of Washington. He spent two years doing graduate work at the University of Nevada where he founded the *West Coast Poetry Review.*

Ransom's stories have appeared in *Out of Sight, Mojo Navigator(e), Port Townsend Journal,* and *Gamut;* his poems in *New York Quarterly, Ironwood, the goodly co, Paintbrush, Port Townsend Journal, New Mexico Magazine,* and others. A collection of his poetry, *Finding True North,* was published by Copper Canyon Press and has been nominated for the Pulitzer Prize and the National Book Award. A special illustrated edition of *Critter* will be published by the Edge Press in New Zealand.

He is currently at work on a novel and has spent the past two years as Poet in Residence for the Washington State Arts Commission and the National Endowment for the Arts. He lives with his wife, Kathy, and their daughter, Hali Kalae, on a small farm on the Olympic Peninsula in Washington.

Critter

I

Of the secret of the Grail,
he commits a great sin and a great wrong
who undertakes to tell the tale
otherwise than as it should run.

—Bleheris

Sat up all night and lugged at the moon.
Grunted. Nothing changed.
Sun rolled up the mountain.
I could tell about
meadowlarks, finches
or dogwood and poplar,
madronas, cedar—
no, it was Orion I waited for.
Orion and the whisper of a lug,
lug-lug, lug-lug
from the deep black ages
past his light.

Shed on the highway at twilight,
Lured and ate a slow raven—
he fluttered, lost his feathers
but did not change, tasted muddy.
Red-bearded man in a van camped nearby.
Had a dog and a newly pregnant wife.
Eyed him across the moonlight.
Even the leaves stopped breathing.
He withered under his beard,
bright eyes filled his face.
"Lug-lug, lug-lug," and the moonlight
pushed itself across the van
And the man, the van, the dog
the newly pregnant wife were gone.

A soft pause.
Stretched out in the clearing
and slept.
Stretched the clearing around my moulting fur,
and slept.

Orion whirled and pulled,
spun himself through clouds,
twisted and rolled
West to mint, firs,
grandfather cedars and sea.

Woke before dawn.
Three bone-suckers snuffled my toes,
my crotch, back of my neck.
Coyotes carry ticks in rotten fur,
never die fat.
I draw coyotes like a lump of ripe carrion.
Sighed.
They slid away like gray desert otters.
Night otters.
They would see this place again,
shadow-place, empty.
They would follow a strong scent,
melt West through blue sage and pinion pine.

Critters found a log bridge
from Orion to Wyoming.
Seven crossed.
Bridge slipped, snapped,
spilled critters across light,
across time.
Seven lugged and wept.
Laid up three hundred winters
in dry rock caves,
ate small bats and sour toads.

Watched for signs, slept lightly,
died slowly
one by one.

Watched them weaken.
Watched them cough, spit, shudder.
Watched them watch me,
watch the moon,
watch Orion.
Watched their fur glaze with dust,
watched their eyes glaze with light,
watched them die.
One by one by one.
There are more numbers
than leaves, than stones,
than stars.
Only one is sad.
One terrifies one terrified.
Only one.

Tired Critter lay on a rock.
Ringed by soft fires outside,
rung by soft hymns inside,
Critter prayed for Critter,
slept again, belly up
head on rock.

Rain.
Hard wind, stinging rain.
Storm swept like a fat black hand
down bluffs, down alleys,
snuffed streets, homes, lights.
Spirits moaned,
canyons wept.
Critter clutched a slick wet cliff
and slept.

II

If a man loses anything
and goes back
and looks carefully for it
he will find it.

—Tatanka Yotanka
(Sitting Bull)

River sounds.
River and rustling trees.
Looked out on green, green,
river and green.
Two drakes whistled by
like breath from old nostrils.
They turned, turned,
their steady black eyes my eyes.
They dove into sunrise
melting, rippling
down-canyon, downwind.

I am a heap of compost,
a pile of last year's leaves
mulched through desert
blown into mountains
somehow intact.
O Orion! this country,
this star has a magic, too.

Couldn't stand.
Brittle bones locked, ached.
Crawled slowly to water.
Rested, drank.
Silver-green leaves vibrating,
twirling by thousands,
by hundreds of thousands around,

all around, all up and down river,
confused, made Critter dizzy.
Crawled back against a mossy bank,
shut bleary eyes, shut out flocks of leaves.
Chewed twigs and buds,
smelled damp pine,
roots, river rocks.
Smelled man.

Looked up, careful.
Red-bearded man.
Red-bearded man sat upstream,
watching, chewing grass.
Eyed me across the clearing.
"Picked you up in the desert,
brought you here.
There's water here.
My home is here."
Lugged.
"You'll be all right," he said.
Like he was talking to a child,
talking to a pet.
Told his wife he found a Sasquatch.
Tracked me for months.
Lug.

Ate scraps from his porch,
cowed his dog, avoided his wife.
He walked at dawn, talked quietly,
talked and talked.
She waddled heavy, flat-footed
across the garden, stringy hair
hiding hard mouth, hungry teeth.
Cleared her throat and spat.
Twisted her small pale mouth
at me, and spat.

"You are ugly, ugly."
And she threw stones.
"You are a lump of garbage."
Stones.
"You smell like an outhouse."
More stones.

Ran up the road,
lumbered along the road
panted and cringed,
hid in a stand of scrub pine.
Hid like a yak
in a low stand of cabbage.

Sunset.
Rheumatic Critter slogged upstream,
river-numb legs,
sun-numb face,
foolish old mind, tired.
Tired old mind saw white,
heard cries, pain.
Stood above the pass
above the long, long
sun-red lake.
Saw blood, saw white.
Tired old mind saw
frozen eyes,
hungry eyes, empty.
Looked West, across the lake
across the pass.
Looked down.
Tired old mind saw white,
saw blood,
saw men eating men,
saw black.

III

Within the bier was a body,
And without, on the silk,
There lay a sword
Which was broken in the middle.

—Chretien

Critter dreams upside-down.
Critter dreams inside-out,
backwards.
Man floats by,
white,
bound around
wrapped all around in white.
Bumps Critter,
turns once like a cracked leaf
on a still pond,
bumps Critter,
stops.

Tried to move, to turn.
Tried to lug, lug-lug.
Tried to open crusty eyes,
roll,
squirm out of sleep.
Slid deep, deep.

Thick black boots peeling mud
flop like dead chickens,
drop out of sight.
A burned, twisted twig
swells, crawls toward Critter,
cold, sweaty Critter.

Twisted branch sprouts
bright brass buds,
bright smooth barrel,
blood groove,
steel.
Nicks Critter's nose,
belly, genitals.
Tickles Critter's thighs, knees,
swollen, throbbing feet.
Hovers low above,
cocks,
stands easy.

Seven women in black and red,
seven dark, weeping women
carry corn and strips of cloth,
fish bones, sand, sea shell bracelets,
obsidian knives and dried moss.
Moaning women step slowly, circle the corpse,
chant strange rhythms in high, quivering voices.

Critter smells corn silk
and sweet, bursting kernels.
Hears heavy stalks groan
into each other, scrape,
whistle their high, growing sounds
across the dark.

Critter sees seven women
chanting, swaying, shuffling
a soft circle around, around.
Their feet are the sound
of stunted corn dying in the sun.
Their eyes are the hollow ends
of cracked bones.

Women turn in their dance,
turn slowly, slowly.
Their hands are stretched
their tears are blood
their cheeks are bone
their bones are dust
their dust is fine,
soft and fine,
blows thick around
close around my helpless head.
Critter thrashes, smothers.
Old Critter chokes.
Dust covers Critter lightly,
holds him down, pats him,
smooths his sleep,
soothes and smooths his twisted sleep.

IV

Life is the breath of a buffalo
in the winter time.
It is the little shadow
which runs across the grass
and loses itself in the Sunset.

—Crowfoot

Soft wet cloth cooled my face,
cleaned thick, numb lips,
crusty nose, eyes.
Red-bearded man lifted my head,
gave me water.
"They're hunting you."
Croaked a lug.
"I covered your tracks.
You'll have to hide."

Looked past him, West.
Saw the black back of the lake
ripple like fur,
ripple like muscle
in a black bear's flank.

"Old One,
what have you seen?"
Like a crippled gelding
downwind from a mare
Critter dreamed, snorted,
dreamed again.
Saw a brown mouse
come out of the south,
follow a twitching nose
through grass, alfalfa, corn husks.
Mouse into leaves, into earth.

Mouse into grass, into earth.
Mouse into moss, into earth.
Brown into green, into earth.
Wide mouse eyes follow
twitching nose,
sleep dreamless sleep.

"Old One,
can you help us?"
Groaned, sat up.
Lugged.
Red-bearded man listened.
Sat quietly, head cocked,
listened.
Critter lugged and lugged,
lugged and wept.
Critter moaned, grunted,
drew in dirt,
arranged twigs and stones.

Red-bearded man stood,
walked around, chewed grass.
"I don't understand."
Lugged.
"I'll lead them away,
give you time."
Lugged.
The sun was up.
Red-bearded man was gone.

Looked backwards, Eastward,
into the sun.
Watched an eagle rise,
swing into the sun, a yellow torch
rising higher, circling above all,

above sun, lake, pass,
above Critter, earth,
above all.

Lugged at the sun.
Grunted. Nothing changed.
Night rolled up the mountain.
It was Orion I waited for.
Orion and the whisper of a lug,
lug-lug, lug-lug
from the deep black ages
past his light.

Saw Orion rise in the North sky
like a one-horned buffalo.
Saw him turn, shake himself.
Saw his white mane scatter
seven sisters like quail.
Saw him paw, snort, hook Andromeda.
Saw him trample stars, clouds, men.
Saw his breath
in the cold Northern night.
Saw the bottoms of his eyes.
Saw white.

Message from Ohanapecosh Glacier

I have seen the soft light flicker,
seen the nose and fingers pressed flat,
fogging the ice at my feet, sinking.
That is no spirit.
Chants echo white in her deep eyes,
blackening visions shift hourly above her face.
She is never dry.
Put your ear to the ice:
a long, stuttering groan.
She is blue, arthritic, naked.
She hunts a lover.
Leave everything here.
Her trail is this twisting stream
that she sends, milky, to the sea.

Statement on Our Higher Education

for Ron Lampard, Nisqually

We learned that you don't shoot
things that are wiser than yourself:
cranes, crippled bear, mountain beaver, toads.
We learned that a hunter who doesn't eat his game
is a traitor and should wander the earth,
starving, forever.
We learned to fish the shadow side of creeks
and to check traps every morning before the dew lifts.
It is a kindness in our savagery
that we learned to owe our prey
a clean death and an honorable end.
We learned from our game
to expect to be eaten when we die,
learned that our fathers
learned all this before us.
Because of this you are brother
to cranes, mountain beaver, toads and me.
And to one old crippled bear
that neither of us will ever see.

Indian Summer: Montana, 1956

for Gene Left Hand

Not in my saddle, but above it.
"Even eagles have to land," I thought.
My right cheek twitched down:
leather, blister, bruise, bone.
Up again.
My thighs were tight humming wires.
My uncle's foaming roan muscled smoothly
into your uncle's Appaloosas mare.
I could have been more excited.

After noon we bucked bales
to our own long slow rhythm.
My raw hands made riding in easy.

That night, after burning black ticks
out of our glowing burnt hides,
you kicked the fire down, looked up
and said, "We came from there."
You slept safely in a whirl of stars.
At daybreak I chose a longer, dustier way home.

On the Morning of the Third Night
Above Nisqually

Images drip down my back like sweat.
From this hunger I can see time.
Dreams float in deep green whirls under that fog.
Four brown bears stepped through,
mist washing around them like steam
or old reluctant spirits.
We bowed in a ritual I did not know I knew.
A white woman stumbled slowly past
children bent her long pale back.
Her blue eyes opened like the sun
and two white scars sunk through my chest.
The bears shuffled close, shook their manes
and waved their heavy arms against her.
She dropped the children and they grew like gods.
Bear smell thickened, they backed around me like walls.
She touched the bears and they were stone.
She stacked them down there by the creek,
her children standing guard like pillars
and her breasts hanging golden in the sun.
She lumbers up the hill, low to the ground,
her hot skin wet under mud and matted fur.
Tonight she comes for me.

Grandpa's .45

Lifting, both hands pulling whitely.
How did Hoppy do it one-handed every Saturday?
Grandpa cocks it: tic tic.
Blinking like a startled lizard
in some green rain cobweb swamp
I squeeze, and shake, and squeeze.

I am deaf, floating on my skinny back
in choking swirls of bark and burnt powder.

". . . it it."

I'm up on one elbow, blurring.
Dad's there, by the stump, laughing.
"Be goddamned, he hit it."
And as he points out the neat, off-center hole,
as he laughs the very first laugh I remember him laughing,
I brush my watery eyes, and breathe.

Catechism, 1958

She hovered hooded, blue-eyed:
"What happens to those souls
who take their own lives?"
Your eyes inspected your desk, hopelessly.
"Stand when called upon!"
Your so-white hands
shook like ginkgo leaves,
breathless tears moved you slowly to the door.
I sat, quiet as packed dirt.
"If you leave this room
keep on going."
Years behind those flooded eyes
your father dangled like a burnt moth
from a noose in our old tree house.

Both of us kept on going.

Wendy Rose

Wendy Rose was born in 1948. She is half Hopi and has lived both on reservations and in the San Francisco Bay Area.

She attended Contra Costa College, where she founded the Native American Student Union, and is currently studying at the University of California at Berkeley. She is co-founder of the Light of Dawn Temple, a metaphysical research center, and served as a staff writer and cover artist for *Many Smokes* magazine.

A painter as well as a writer, Rose has sold her work throughout the Far West.

For Anita Endrezze Probst

For W. M. Ransom

Poem to a Redskin

In the Seminole darkness of your singing eyes,
the sunset amber-glow streams &
    In the Seminole darkness of your shadows &
in the sunstroke words you speak &
    In the Seminole darkness in your hand that hides
between body & junebug wings &
    In the Seminole darkness of torn geographies
that litter the swamp of your thighs &
    In the Seminole darkness that whispers to me
what light-headed spirit interfered &
    In the Seminole darkness of your smile
at my asking of names & at your reply
    that you were anyone I wished, so
I just whispered back that the Seminole must
    also feel Kachina.

Oh Father

for C.L.

Oh father, now that i have touched
your hand,
> fingertips melting each into the other,
> spirits merging

two eagles excited into flight, fire into fire,
earth wet with earth;
oh father, now that i have found
a new strength,
> inside your eyes, tremendous panorama
> mesa and river and—

all i have to do is look into your eyes . . .

Pottery shards, splintered and dusty,
glued together by that which is spirit
—may it someday hold water—

My questions a marathon of
jackrabbits by your ears;
i'm sorry i guess
but i have to know:

oh father, who am i?

For Walter Lowenfels

Shall we have a family born
of kitchen cloves   a scent
on sutured winds racing
thru windows in knotty-pine palaces
merely shrugging
to feel the wind squeeze thru?
                laughter always
as I had imagined it
with imaginary fathers before.
                the one who stroked my
                sixteen-year-old mind as it flashed
                in chaos, all directions at once,
                to end on a redwood and squat crying;
                or the one thinking himself the elder brother
                who held in his cupped hands the eighteen year old
                my constant shadow out of step;
                or the odd coincidence forever feathering
                my ear—a real father somewhere hiding,
                absorbed into silver with teeth turning to
                coral.
& now along comes Walter—
the lamp post seems tuned to your key.

Celebration for My Mother

Tickled,
my thoughts wander
through the whys and wherefores
of your hollybranch life,
yet wonder where it all began,
when now I see it ending;

watch you looking somewhere else, shut down,
nibbling at your mud-foot,
brushing the cat hairs from your lap.
I perspired in your world twenty-five years
and think I could have known better
than to roll heavily on the perimeter
of ethnic pride. I deserve to die with the grace
of each question forming in my eyes
that are darker than yours, and wider.

Am I really more open than you?
Or is your radiant virtue, the locking inside
oneself, harmless and quiet, one I missed?
Yet, it did affect the escaping light
about my mind, growing away from you.
And your leafing through my life's work
like last week's news was a little painful;

but I couldn't share the pain with you,
there in our separate hiding rooms.
I try not to lose that tiny thread
connecting happy to sad.
So, my thoughts remain iridescent
and tender when I reach the question
I send blowing through your hair:
please believe in me.

To an Imaginary Father

for Walter

it was said at the
flirting creekwater's birth
in the backyard of a berkeley house
—she looks just like her daddy
changing colors in the night—

& it was there
i began to dream
of a birdhouse blowing
in summer, a sunstorm
falling,
a milkweed letter on my
lap of cats

& yes i saw the
magpie shed her feathers
on your cheek
to place an emerald
where the tear had lain.

& myself found shouting
how it's my life &
liberty; how i might choose
hanging black hair & a void
watching Kachinas weep crystal   .
to slap the red-brown pretzel child
needing a father to claim her.

& twenty-four years later
wrote Walter
twenty-four years late.

Saint Patrick's Day, 1973

sure an' twas a

fine st. patrick's day
with its waxing moon an'

dead lilies;
sure an' the sun rose on time

for once turning clouds clockwise
& trying not to rain;

earth is putty-soft,
dents too easily.

in the night i watched
my scars,

by themselves a city
grown dense on my hips,

my back, my breast, everywhere hard hands
have slashed . . . yet, these keep to themselves

& disturb
no one; the frail spiderweb of scars

in my mind is
the enemy of light; the dark density

reminding me forever
to duck,

the daily flight
at my senses of these couplets.

Oh My People I Remember

Oh my People, I remember that dream.
It came as I walked, awake yet sleeping,
hands pocketed for slim slivers of
warmth—
Mainland then and the vision saw me
walking.
Touched on the shoulder, my eyes ascended
and down, as though black lead,
they saw—myriads of hands,
pyramids of faces, and
it was you, my People, it was you!
You reached out to me.
Forming a circle, a sacred Hoop, I felt
protected—within the Mother/Father.
But as I walked, laying within the vision's belly,
in this fellowship I saw, confused and
unbelieving, it was I holding them up
and I was also held.
Why me? I asked. More rational: How?
Neither leader nor fullblood,
how and why me?

*** Do not bury such plagues
      upon our bodies—we are One
      and you are One with us ***

Grateful, daring at last to believe,
I walked sentry awhile more and
turning, the vision stayed.

Oh my People
walking within this sunset
on our ALCATRAZ—
I have not forgotten.

Self Dirge

for Don

My hair has dried
the mind of my wind;
I watched the shrinking
of calloused will, of music
weaving into holy sirens
of hurt where hurt is

I knew the what-of-everything
before I was born;
before my life a nirvana of its own.
Before life a mirror to be born . . .

. . . why dark, cold,
insatiable wet? my own face
the trap of a path on which
I walk into fences
wet

                good morning
                balalaika
                good morning
                drum song
        Did I step on your music
        tracing fish-ferns?
        Did I blow down the barriers
        keeping atom from atom
        throughout these walls
        elongating silence?
and why pain?

America

give me a color
to step in,
a color for my
table, a color to thrash
my hands in—
my inner swirls
are grey with yesterday's promises
becoming today's raining wail.

I want only to lightly touch
the dividers in your hand,
to shove a finger thru the veiling
that stands by you:
afraid even to need
its own master.

So when they push us
into the cave again,
I'll cover my anguish
with Old Woman's shawl
and give them back
their eyelessness.

For Steph

(on the occasion of Ralph's death)

i am not blind
i see your soul bulldozed
under,
i see its edges becoming
more & more a
hard core of edges,
i see the free tears
begin to freeze

        feeling maybe hurried
        or inspected yet
        lazy tho' they know
        they've only reached a

breathing space &
must finish their
falling,
i see the gold-glitter coaldust
billow, hardening, on your
shoulders that sometimes forget
themselves & shake,
i see the chestnut blanket
hair, finest natural macramé,
lose track of itself
& let go

      streaming in pieces
      & tangled,

i see you counting your
blemishes, knowing the contradictions
of beauty
as the one who taught you the
resolutions has

beautified himself all the way
to a tin-feathered
casket
      blowing kisses from an
      increasing distance.

They Sometimes Call Me

they sometimes call me
seller of second-hand visions
not having known
the fever of small moths
resting quietly in their marrow
& fluttering past
insignificant dreams
like they were the bread
of a wise man & plum cider.

the priceless visions
in the crook of my elbow
are only pebbles
chickens have scratched
searching
for the commoner
majesty of sand
& not for sale at all.

For My People

i was myself blown
two leafs apart
(seeing the ground swim within
sliding and slipping together
and apart)

growing closer
biting at our shadows
loving on our feet
dying in our souls
losing one another . . .
losing ourselves

finding

Grunion

trembling, sand-dollar
blows sand through sky—
dark and underground hinges—as if
nothing were important enough
to die for

the grunion are building
a star tunnel

Epitaph

The roots of mankind are tangled in my hair,
and the leaves (brownblack brittle) blind my eyes.

Tell me, phoenix,
is rebirth such a beautiful bird?

Leslie Silko

Leslie Silko was born in 1948 in Albuquerque, New Mexico. She was brought up on the Laguna Pueblo reservation and is part Laguna, part Plains Indian, and part white. Her search for identity as a half-breed is, she says, at the core of her writing.

Silko graduated from the University of New Mexico and studied for three semesters at that university's American Indian Law Program before leaving to devote herself full-time to writing fiction and poetry. She lives with her husband and two sons in Ketchikan, Alaska.

Toe'osh: A Laguna Coyote Story

for Simon Ortiz, July 1973

I

In the wintertime
at night
we tell coyote stories
                    and drink Spañada by the stove.
How coyote got his
ratty old fur coat
                    bits of old fur
                    the sparrows stuck on him
                    with dabs of pitch.
That was after he lost his proud original one in a poker game.
Anyhow, things like that
are always happening to him,
that's what she said, anyway.

And it happened to him at Laguna
and Chinle
and at Lukachukai too, because coyote got too smart for his own
    good.

II

But the Navajos say he won a contest once.
It was to see who could sleep out in a
snow storm the longest
and coyote waited until chipmunk badger and skunk were all
curled up under the snow
and then he uncovered himself and slept all night
inside
and before morning he got up and went out again
and waited until the others got up before he came
in to take the prize.

                                    Leslie Silko   223

III

Some white men came to Acoma and Laguna a hundred years ago
and they fought over Acoma land and Laguna women, and even now
some of their descendants are howling
in the hills southeast of Laguna.

IV

Charlie Coyote wanted to be governor
and he said that when he got elected
he would run the other men off
the reservation
and keep all the women for himself.

V

One year
the politicians got fancy
at Laguna.
They went door to door with hams and turkeys
and they gave them to anyone who promised
to vote for them.
On election day all the people
stayed home and ate turkey
and laughed.

VI

The Trans-Western pipeline vice president came
to discuss right-of-way.
The Lagunas let him wait all day long
because he is a busy and important man.
And late in the afternoon they told him
to come back again tomorrow.

VII

They were after the picnic food
that the special dancers left
down below the cliff.
And *Toe'osh* and his cousins hung themselves
down over the cliff
holding each other's tail in their mouth making a coyote chain
until someone in the middle farted
and the guy behind him opened his
mouth to say "What stinks?" and they
all went tumbling down, like that.

VIII

Howling and roaring
Toe'osh scattered white people
out of bars over Wisconsin.
He bumped into them at the door
until they said
       "Excuse me"
And the way Simon meant it
was for 300 or maybe 400 years.

Prayer to the Pacific

I

I traveled to the ocean
    distant
        from my southwest land of sandrock
        to the moving blue water
    Big as the myth of origin.

II

Pale
pale water in the yellow-white light of
        sun   floating west
            to China
        where ocean herself was born
Clouds that blow across the sand are wet.

III

Squat in the wet sand and speak to Ocean:
    I return to you turquoise the red coral you sent us,
        sister spirit of Earth.
Four round stones in my pocket   I carry back the ocean
        to suck and to taste.

IV

Thirty thousand years ago
    Indians came riding across the ocean
    carried by giant sea turtles.
Waves were high that day
    great sea turtles waded   slowly   out
        from the grey sundown sea.
Grandfather Turtle rolled in the sand   four times
        and disappeared
        swimming into the sun.

V

And so   from that time
            immemorial
                        as the old people say
rainclouds drift from the west
            gift from the ocean.

VI

Green leaves in the wind
Wet earth on my feet
            swallowing raindrops
                        clear from China.

Poem for Ben Barney

(Early spring, Navajo nation, 1973)

If the time ever came
I would call you
                    and you would come.
To stand on that mountain
                    on top of that mountain in the west.
And I would go to the east
                    stand on the mountain in the east
                    and from our mountain-tops

                    call them.

The meadows and mountains
the winds of the earth
                    dancing spinning whirling
all wrapped in leather tongues.

One-legged antelope in the tree-top swaying
Crow with his chorus singing
                         It has finally come to this
                         All their fine magic
                         It has finally come to this.
Crow and his chorus gesturing
                              at the world around them
                    keeping time to Coyote's drum.

Yet so long as we can summon together
                    with flute song flying in the wind
                    and flute man coming from the distances
                              the instrument heavy in his hands
                              skinsoft tree in flower,
                    leaping and dancing lightly
                    sunshine not yet ended
                              sunshine not yet through.

Indian Song: Survival

I

We went north
        to escape winter
climbing pale cliffs
             we paused   to sleep at the river.

II

Cold water   river cold from the north
I sink my body in the shallow
                sink into sand and cold river water.

III

You sleep in the branches of
            pale river willows above me.
I smell you in the silver leaves, mountainlion man
                green willows aren't sweet enough to hide you.

IV

I have slept with the river and
             he is warmer than any man.
At sunrise
      I heard ice on the cattails.

V

Mountain lion, with dark yellow eyes
            you nibble moon flowers
           while we wait.
I don't ask   why do you come
           on this desperation journey north.

VI

I am hunted for my feathers
I hide in spider's web
           hanging   in a thin grey tree
                   above the river.
In the night   I hear music
           song of branches   dry leaves scraping the moon.

VII

Green spotted frogs sing to the river
                 and   I know he is waiting.
Mountain lion shows me the way
           paths of mountain wind
           climbing higher
                up
                  up to Cloudy Mountain.

VIII

It is only a matter of time, Indian
                  you can't sleep with the river forever.
Smell winter and know.

IX

I swallow black mountain dirt
           while you catch hummingbirds
             trap them with wildflowers
            pollen and petals
             fallen from the Milky Way

X

You lay beside me in the sunlight
        warmth around us and
        you ask me if I still smell winter.
Mountain forest wind travels east and I answer:
        taste me,
           I am the wind
        touch me,
           I am the lean grey deer
        running on the edge of the rainbow.

James Welch

James Welch was born November 18, 1940 in
Browning, Montana. He is Blackfeet on his father's
side and Gros Ventre on his mother's. He attended
schools on the Blackfeet and Fort Belknap reservations
and in Minneapolis, Minnesota. He then attended the
University of Minnesota for one year and Northern
Montana College for two, eventually receiving his B.A.
from the University of Montana.
Welch has worked as a laborer, firefighter, and Up-
ward Bound counselor. He is now writing full time.
His poetry has been published extensively in literary
journals both here and abroad. His first book, a collection of his poems titled *Riding the Earthboy* 40
(World), was published in 1971. His second, a novel
called *Winter in the Blood* (Harper & Row),
was published in 1974. He lives with his wife, Lois, on
a farm outside Missoula, Montana.

Blue like Death

You see, the problem is
no more for the road. Moon fails
in snow between the moon
and you. Your eyes ignite
the way that butterfly
should move had you not killed it
in a dream of love.

The road forked back
and will fork again the day
you earn your lies,
the thrill of being what you are
when shacks begin to move
and coyotes kill the snakes
you keep safe at home in jars.

The girl let you out. She prized
your going the way some people
help a drunk to fall.
Easy does it, one two three
and let him lie. For he was blue
and dirt is where the bones
meet. You met his eyes

out there where the road dips
and children whipped the snake
you called Frank to death
with sticks. Now you understand:
the way is not your going
but an end. That road awaits
the moon that falls between
the snow and you, your stalking home.

The Renegade Wants Words

We died in Zortman on a Sunday
in the square, beneath sky so blue
the eagles spoke in foreign tongues.
Our deeds were numbered: burning homes,
stealing women, wine and gold.

No one spoke of our good side,
those times we fed the hulking idiot,
mapped these plains with sticks
and flint, drove herds of bison wild
for meat and legend. We expected

no gratitude, no mercy on our heads.
But a word—the way we rode
naked across these burning hills.
Perhaps spring breakup made us move
and trust in stars. Ice, not will,

made our women ice. We burned
homes for heat, painted our bodies
in blood. Who can talk revenge?
Were we wild for wanting men to listen
to the earth, to plant only by moons?

In Zortman on a Sunday we died.
No bells, no man in black
to tell us where we failed.
Makeshift hangman, our necks,
noon and the eagles—not one good word.

For Wendy Rose

For Leslie Silko

Across to the Peloponnese

The last decent man alive
died today in Saronis.
No one remembers what he did
or how he came to be so good.

He died today at ten past three,
the final tick of the soccer match.
Shepherds complained of a winter wind,
the butcher laid down his lamb.

Some mothers say he wrote poems,
stunning poems on rare paper
about—you see, they can't be sure,
the man was sadly foreign.

Flies walk against the windowpane.
A dog barks. So sure of itself
the Aegean mocks these mourners
gathered in his room.

Nobody knows how he died
or why—he had no enemies,
no friends, no murderous need
to throw himself against the rocks.

Fishermen light their nets
crude against the Peloponnese.
In Saronis the men are certain
Greece beat herself, not the Turks.

In My First Hard Springtime

Those red men you offended were my brothers.
Town drinkers, Buckles Pipe, Star Boy,
Billy Fox, were blood to bison. Albert Heavy Runner
was never civic. You are white and common.

Record trout in Willow Creek chose me
to deify. My horse, Centaur, part cayuse,
was fast and mad and black. Dandy in flat hat
and buckskin, I rode the town and called it mine.

A slow hot wind tumbled dust against my door.
Fed and fair, you mocked my philosophic nose,
my badger hair. I rolled your deference
in the hay and named it love and lasting.

Starved to visions, famous cronies top Mount Chief
for names to give respect to Blackfeet streets.
I could deny them in my first hard springtime,
but choose amazed to ride you down with hunger.

Surviving

The day-long cold hard rain drove
like sun through all the cedar sky
we had that late fall. We huddled
close as cows before the bellied stove.
Told stories. Blackbird cleared his mind,
thought of things he'd left behind, spoke:

"Oftentimes, when sun was easy in my bones,
I dreamed of ways to make this land."
We envied eagles easy in their range.
"That thin girl, old cook's kid, stripped naked
for a coke or two and cooked her special stew
round back of the mess tent Sundays."
Sparrows skittered through the black brush.

That night the moon slipped a notch, hung
black for just a second, just long enough
for wet black things to sneak away our cache
of meat. To stay alive this way, it's hard. . . .

Arizona Highways

I see her seventeen,
a lady dark, turquoise
on her wrists. The land
astounded by a sweeping rain
becomes her skin. Clouds
begin to mend my broken eyes.

I see her singing by a broken shack,
eyes so black it must be dawn.
I hum along, act sober,
tell her I could love her
if she dressed better, if her father
got a job and beat her more.
Eulynda. There's a name
I could live with. I could
thrash away the nuns, tell them
I adopt this girl, dark,
seventeen, silver on her fingers,
in the name of the father, son,
and me, the holy ghost.
Why not? Mormons do less
with less. Didn't her ancestors
live in cliffs, no plumbing,
just a lot of love and corn?
Me, that's corn, pollen
in her hair. East, south, west, north—
now I see my role—religious.
The Indian politician made her laugh.
Her silver jingled in her throat,
those songs, her fingers busy
on his sleeve. Fathers, forgive me.
She knows me in her *Tchindii* dream,

always a little pale, too much
bourbon in my nose, my shoes
too clean, belly soft as hers.

I'll move on. My schedule
says Many Farms tomorrow, then
on to Window Rock, and finally home,
that weathered nude, distant
as the cloud I came in on.

Harlem, Montana: Just Off the Reservation

We need no runners here. Booze is law
and all the Indians drink in the best tavern.
Money is free if you're poor enough.
Disgusted, busted whites are running
for office in this town. The constable,
a local farmer, plants the jail with wild
raven-haired stiffs who beg just one more drink.
One drunk, a former Methodist, becomes a saint
in the Indian church, bugs the plaster man
on the cross with snakes. If his knuckles broke,
he'd see those women wail the graves goodbye.

Goodbye, goodbye, Harlem on the rocks,
so bigoted, you forget the latest joke,
so lonely you'd welcome a battalion of Turks
to rule your women. What you don't know,
what you will never know or want to learn—
Turks aren't white. Turks are olive, unwelcome
alive in any town. Turks would use
your one dingy park to declare a need for loot.
Turks say bring it, step quickly, lay down and dead.

Here we are when men were nice. This photo, hung
in the New England Hotel lobby, shows them nicer
than pie, agreeable to the warring bands of redskins
who demanded protection money for the price of food.
Now, only Hutterites out north are nice. We hate
them. They are tough and their crops are always good.
We accuse them of idiocy and believe their belief all wrong.

Harlem, your hotel is overnamed, your children
are raggedy-assed but you go on, survive
the bad food from the two cafes and peddle
your hate for the wild who bring you money.
When you die, if you die, will you remember
the three young bucks who shot the grocery up,
locked themselves in and cried for days, we're rich,
help us, oh God, we're rich.

Please Forward

My arms smell good. Think
I'll start a trout farm,
girls tight and finny, quickly
for my saddest worm.
I discovered decades back
days leave you bushed, the stones
in my gall remain pure.

Dearest, they're talking turkey
in Montana. Mt. Olympus gives me
jitters. How can I say—I told them
I was jazz, hot stuff
from the west, carabinieri,
miles to go before I sleep.

Nothing works but wind that sweeps
us cleaner once a year.
I've a new brand of cigarettes,
one puff and drive another nail.
Write me when I feel better.
Like last night, the dust
from the Aegean called up
many poems. Grave mama, I caught
the silliest and it was me.

In My Lifetime

This day the children of Speakthunder
run the wrong man, a saint unable
to love a weasel way, able only to smile
and drink the wind that makes the others go.
Trees are ancient in his breath.
His bleeding feet tell a story of run
the sacred way, chase the antelope naked
till it drops, the odor of run
quiet in his blood. He watches cactus
jump against the moon. Moon is speaking
woman to the ancient fire. Always woman.

His sins were numerous, this wrong man.
Buttes were good to listen from. With thunder
hands his father shaped the dust, circled
fire, tumbled up the wind to make a fool.
Now the fool is dead. His bones go back
so scarred in time, the buttes are young to look
for signs that say a man could love his fate,
that winter in the blood is one sad thing.

His sins—I don't explain. Desperate in my song,
I run these woman hills, translate wind
to mean a kind of life, the children of Speakthunder
are never wrong and I am rhythm to strong medicine.

Going to Remake This World

Morning and the snow might fall forever.
I keep busy. I watch the yellow dogs
chase creeping cars filled with Indians
on their way to the tribal office.
Grateful trees tickle the busy underside
of our snow-fat sky. My mind is right,
I think, and you will come today
for sure, this day when the snow falls.

From my window, I see bundled Doris Horseman,
black in the blowing snow, her raving son,
Horace, too busy counting flakes to hide his face.
He doesn't know. He kicks my dog
and glares at me, too dumb to thank the men
who keep him on relief and his mama drunk.

My radio reminds me that Hawaii calls
every afternoon at two. Moose Jaw is overcast,
twelve below and blowing. Some people. . . .
Listen: if you do not come this day, today
of all days, there is another time
when breeze is tropic and riffs the green sap
forever up these crooked cottonwoods. Sometimes,
you know, the snow never falls forever.

Christmas Comes to Moccasin Flat

Christmas comes like this: Wise men
unhurried, candles bought on credit (poor price
for calves), warriors face down in wine sleep.
Winds cheat to pull heat from smoke.

Friends sit in chinked cabins, stare out
plastic windows and wait for commodities.
Charlie Blackbird, twenty miles from church
and bar, stabs his fire with flint.

When drunks drain radiators for love
or need, chiefs eat snow and talk of change,
an urge to laugh pounding their ribs.
Elk play games in high country.

Medicine Woman, clay pipe and twist tobacco,
calls each blizzard by name and predicts
five o'clock by spitting at her television.
Children lean into her breath to beg a story:

Something about honor and passion,
warriors back with meat and song,
a peculiar evening star, quick vision of birth.
Blackbird feeds his fire. Outside, a quick 30° below.

The Man from Washington

The end came easy for most of us.
Packed away in our crude beginnings
in some far corner of a flat world,
we didn't expect much more
than firewood and buffalo robes
to keep us warm. The man came down
a slouching dwarf with rainwater eyes,
and spoke to us. He promised
that life would go on as usual,
that treaties would be signed, and everyone—
man, woman, and child—would be inoculated
against a world in which we had no part,
a world of money, promise and disease.

Snow Country Weavers

A time to tell you things are well.
Birds flew south a year ago.
One returned, a blue-wing teal
wild with news of his mother's love.

Mention me to friends. Say
wolves are dying at my door,
the winter drives them from their meat.
Say this: say in my mind

I saw your spiders weaving threads
to bandage up the day. And more,
those webs were filled with words
that tumbled meaning into wind.

D-Y Bar

The tune is cowboy; the words, sentimental crap.
Farther out, wind is mending sagebrush,
stapling it to earth in rows only a badger
would recommend. Reservoirs are dry,
the sky commands a cloud high
to skip the Breaks bristling with heat
and stunted pine.

In stunted light, Bear Child tells a story
to the mirror. He acts his name out,
creeks muscling gorges fill his glass
with gumbo. The bear crawls on all fours
and barks like a dog. Slithering snake-wise
he balances a nickel on his nose. The effect,
a snake in heat.

We all know our names here. Summer is a poor
season to skip this place or complain
about marauding snakes. Often when wind
is cool off mountains and the flats
are green, cars stop for gas, motors clicking
warm to songs of a junction bar, head down,
the dormant bear.

Magic Fox

They shook the green leaves down,
those men that rattled
in their sleep. Truth became
a nightmare to their fox.
He turned their horses into fish,
or was it horses strung
like fish, or fish like fish
hung naked in the wind?

Stars fell upon their catch.
A girl, not yet twenty-four
but blonde as morning birds, began
a dance that drew the men in
green around her skirts.
In dust her music jangled memories
of dawn, till fox and grief
turned nightmare in their sleep.

And this: fish not fish but stars
that fell into their dreams.

Why I Didn't Go to Delphi

My feet taste funny
in this light.
Flowers tell me nothing.
Was it all a dream,
a morning made by birds
sailing to Glyfada, dodging
caiques, red breezes
north from Africa?

Nikos drove that west sea
wild with explanations
of demotic songs, Count Basie,
goat feet tender to the cliff.

I believed that slapstick chin,
old gestures of disdain,
older gestures of the knife
slicing off that final breath
of fifteen-day-old lambs.

The butcher looked up,
startled. His mother
brought a basin of water.
Reflected off Hymettus,
the sea changed to asphodel.
Children who could not speak
spoke, and that sad oracle
wild with premonition,
for the seventh time
explained the origin of death.

Directions to the Nomad

Past the school and down
this little incline—
you can't miss it.
Tons of bricks and babies
blue from the waist down.
Their heads are cheese
and loll as though
bricks became their brains.

What's that—the noble savage?
He's around, spooked and colored
by the fish he eats,
red for rainbow, blue
for the moon. He instructs stars,
but only to the thinnest wolf.

When you get there
tell the mad decaying creep
we miss him. We never
meant it. He'll treat you right,
show you poems
the black bear couldn't dream.
One more thing—if he tries
to teach you mountains
or whisper imagined love
to the tamarack, tell him
you adore him,
then get the hell out, fast.

Verifying the Dead

We tore the green tree down
searching for my bones.
A coyote drove the day back
half a step until we killed
both him and it. Our knives
became a bed for quick things.
It's him, all right
I heard old Nine Pipe say.
As we turned away,
a woman blue as night
stepped from my bundle
rubbed her hips and sang
of a country, like this, far off.

Ray A. Young Bear

Ray A. Young Bear was born in Tama, Iowa, in 1950. His tribe is Sauk and Fox of Iowa, better known as the Mesquakies. He has been writing since 1966 and says he begins by thinking in his native Mesquaki and then translating his thoughts into English.

His work has appeared in numerous magazines and anthologies, including *Northwest Poetry Review* and *American Poetry Review* and will be included in a forthcoming anthology from Viking Press.

Young Bear lives with his wife, Stella, and plans to resume studies of art and literature in the fall of 1974.

These Horses Came

I

from inside the bird a dream hums itself out and turns
into sky-wind rushing over my face that needs
a small feather from the otter's nose to blow away
and create corners where i will stand
and think myself into hard ways.

II

these horses came on light grey clouds
and carried off the barbed wire fence-post.
i started thinking about a divided bird
in four pieces of blood in winters hunt
with this certain song rolling the day westward.
the snow falls in one direction and loses me
as i breathe the whiteness like magic.

III

the railroad tracks steal a distance
makes me forget which way
the eager crows are singing/low against the quiet.
in my dream-eye came her words and reminded
me of a story i once fell asleep to.

i aim my rifle cautiously at the sun
and ask: are you really afraid of children?

Star Blanket

the cracks on the walls
of the summer house
divides the earth into pieces
of blue knots on a string.

we are in night
as it is outside.
sightless, i grow
into my patients,
arrange them in the order
of their warmth.

the sound of bird.
its wings.
the flexing of my bones
makes the beans shake
by the woman's feet.
a single leg begins to move,
gets up and fits itself
over the cracks.

i see whistles
catching and eating
the gourds as they spin
and talk on the dirt
floor, nudging everyone away
from their boundaries.

with my fingers together,
a man loops leather
around them, tying them
to his.
inside the star blanket,
i hear the wind slapping
the canvas over the roof.

the intensity of light
is felt and everyone grows
concerned, appoints
the door-faced man
to climb to the roof,
covering the night
more securely.

at my feet,
a row of sitting men
are level like trees.
i hear their wings,
sounding hollow,
filled with conversation,
boring a hole in the sky.
the smell of wood
everywhere.

swallowing a small copper
tube, i light up the people's
bodies and detect blood clots
travelling freely like worms.

the tube brings back
the sickness while i grind
the red rock with my teeth
into sand, mixing it into
the grey and blue holes
of the woman's inner skin,
patching her bag of busting
water.

as the tube goes out
again, i feel the mouth
of a baby attaching itself
to the tube, blowing its
heart back and forth,
gesturing to me,
depressed with the one name
it has.

i fit my heart on one end
and breathe out of the copper
his name: two men lying
to the third.

The Way the Bird Sat

even for the wind there was no room.
the wind kept the cool to itself
and it seemed that his skin
also grew more selfish to feelings
for he was like a window
jealous of the light going through
denied his shadow the sun's warmth
when being alone brought him
the cool.

the way the bird sat
dividing the weather through songs
cleaning the snow and rain
from the underside of its wings
was evidence.
in its singing the bird counted
and acknowledged the changes
in the coolness of the wind.
he somehow held the bird responsible
as it flew about taking in puffs
of air.

often the image of blue hearts
in the form of deer crossed his mind
outdoing all magic and distortion
of the hummingbird who had previously
been the source of his dreams to follow.

now his thoughts took him out
into a cornfield where he felt himself
bundled up concerned about the deer
and their hearts.
the hummingbird who had been dodging

the all-day rain stopped
and hovered beside him
before it flew off
licking the rain from the trees.

having killed and eaten so many deer
it was wrong to blame his weakness
on the sun and wind.
to accuse anyone nearby he thought
was foolish as the consideration
to once save his morning's spit
with the intention of showing it
to people as proof that his blood
and time were almost out.
he even wanted to ask
if it was possible to leave it behind
for worship but all this faded away
like the flutter of wings
he always heard shooting past
the shadow of his foot before it
touched the ground.

once his nose bled all day
and he saved the blood
testing to see if his notions were true.
he allowed the blood to run into a cup
until the cup collected.
towards evening he emptied
the cups in the yard
and just before the sun left
the standing forms of blood glistened.
when he woke he found
his blood missing.
his dog looked content with blood
along the rim of his mouth.

there was nothing but dark spots
on the grass:

the daylight was full and the birds
walked through his yard
speaking to each other
and sometimes gathering
around the area where he had set
his blood.

it was strange as he watched.
each time they walked away
from the area it was smooth
and directed.
in his mind it reminded him
of a ceremony and he left lines
of where each bird had stepped
where each had circled
what words it might have said
even the prayers it might have sung
and when the birds had sticks
in their mouths he saw singers
with their notched sticks.
their beaks moved up and down
the sticks making a rasping noise
and when they hummed
it was a song he knew very well.
he danced to the rhythm
as he watched from the window.
the birds had faces of people
he had met and lost
but there was one he could not recognize
its face was of a deer.
he felt puzzled licking the rain
from the trees.

In Dream: The Privacy of Sequence

always expecting the winter
to be a sad one
i slept after heavy eating of food
and waited until the portions
grew alive.
they sprouted antlers and formed
into circles,
fitted themselves perfectly
into my hollow teeth
and spoke to each other
in comfort about the quiet welcome
they were to receive:
of imitating the distance
between the sky, earth
and the children
shaping a figure from the snow,
recognized and visible
in the eyes of old people
quickly running to their trunks
and fires,
unrolling the contracted faces
of relatives:
long trails of smoke streamed out
from the houses that rested
deep inside the hills.
trees stood about with their arms
stretched out over their foreheads
blocking out the sun,
wondering why the children's laughter
at that moment
seemed to cover everything
in the whole valley including sound.

the trees turned to the old man
who had been sitting in front
of the sun.
the old man right away thought
he knew the reason why the trees' eyes
closed when he met them with his.
repositioning himself, he pretended
to gaze out past them
into the valley.
relieved, he whistled like a bird
and then suddenly realized
much more the quietness
that was in the air.
without birds or leaves
or anything to travel in the wind with
except his acknowledgement
which went from tree to tree
being refused at each ear.

feeling strange, he stood up
and saw for the first time
children running in the open
with kites in their hands.
the old man was familiar
with the faces in the sky
and once in his dream
these were actually disguised gods,
infected birds who lowered
their guts to the mouths of children.
everyone died because of kites.

outside, the depicted visitor
standing as the weather
gathers itself around me
holding in each hand

strings of dried hearts,
the coming hardship of death.
with a mouthful of ashes,
he digs into the earth
hoping to save his warmth
for the dog who sleeps without dreams
or without me to stand above him,
reminding him of the cold
and the dark thin birds
inside my stomach.
his memory of blood tied in little bags.

forgetting the good
of the coming spring,
my fingernails grew long
like brittle shovels
and dug out the squirrel
and pheasant from my teeth,
thick and warm, resembling rocks.
afraid of the daylight
they only came out halfway
from the earth.
i wanted to protect them.
i thought only of their outcome.
i thought of ways to deceive
the dark thin birds speckled
through the sky, wearing masks.
i thought that whoever took
to their air would eventually
stop in flight and then decay,
afraid that it would be my
own howling that i would hear
out in the open
mixed with the talking deer.
the deer who sometimes laugh

while skinning a man after a day's hunt.
their fingers poking through the path
of the bullet, tracing the clot.
the head left behind for the people
in the woods.

i found myself between the airs
of changing weather
unable to distinguish
what to kill, layers of wind over my eyes,
growing old and uncertain,
cutting out the kneeling children
linked together by arms
and thrown to the dog
who refuses though he knows
it is a worship to his skill
and lets the others eat.

once, a boy with puffed-up eyes
took out the roof of his mouth
and sharpened his knife
on his heart,
licked the knife and smiled,
carved me a boat
with arms and legs.
all night, the boat struggled to lift
its burnt belly to the stars.
sensing that the boy had fallen asleep,
daylight came,
took the boy's knife and sliced
off the boy's fingers,
crushed them, dried and sifted them
with its hands and breath
until they were trees.
the particles that blew away

from the daylight's warm breath
made the boy dream
that he had rubbed his hands
against the sky.

For James Welch

For Ray A. Young Bear

Waiting to Be Fed

She swam smiling in the river
thinking it was good that she
had come here to be with the sun
going out into the air
and giving warmth to her sisters' faces
watching her from the sides
listening carefully for the hum
of human voices.
no one would show up here today
she thought. it was too hot
to swim with the sun
radiating on the wings of insects
flying back and forth
between shadow and sunlight
confused in their decisions
evident by the sound
of their open mouths everywhere.

through the years to now
she had known the river well.
sometimes she imagined herself
a rock under the water
surrounded by a landscape
that would bend the trees
through the sky
and then through the stars
reminding her of burnt holes
in cloth that protected
her hand from fire
while cooking for people
waiting to be fed.
she knew a place where
it was like this

where it suddenly became cool
and clear. this place
had often been mentioned
in her mother's constant warnings
about rivers.
like the insects and the sunlight
she released her thought
to a spiderweb drifting
across the river
breaking through the clouds
losing all revenge to the giants
lifting their heads in their watch
to her swimming over the cool
gushing spring
coming up from under the river
thinking of her stomach
and how it was growing fast.
the child swimming inside her:
the touching and speaking of two hearts
made her feel she could smell the sweetness
of the baby's skin in her breath.

in time she would be able to see
the face inside her stomach.
a dream indented on her body.
she took care of it
as if it were a god
as if the snow in winter
had already begun to take shape
in the hands of children
far from the staring foreheads
of their houses.
she knew it wasn't sacred
but everything in the land
seemed that way.

everyone took great interest
and care for her that she
could somehow make out visible
strips of gentleness gathering
around her body
streaming out from her family
a circle of suns.

she looked at the reflection
of her eyes floating over the water.
the water blended with the rustling of leaves.
her sisters broke her thoughts
when they suddenly nodded
down to the sky in agreement
with the flashing on their faces.
she quickly asked if there
was anything wrong
but they remained motionless
eyes looking tricked in sleep
until she found herself
shouting and hitting
at the water all sound returning.
released from spell
they smiled and remarked
to the sand how beautiful
the drawings were.
the turtles carved into trees.
each stood and examined
the sand carefully
their hands moving about
in discussion.

she felt her body drifting away
taken by the foam
and the mouths of carp

in search of tunneling insects.
the water rippled to the banks
and the mud formed bubbles
in response.
each time one popped
a sharp bark shattered
her sisters' bodies into pieces.
in the water she could hear
the clicking of teeth.
the trees limped to her.
the mud rose and made itself
into several seals.
the seals running to her sisters
and devouring them.
all trees and grasses leaned
away from the river
as soon as the seals
jumped into the river
with their arms pointing at her
gesturing each other on.

she felt twisted in a dream.
there was talk around her
and she could sense by their words
that it was night and that
relatives were inside the room
being fed.
each one chewing and then
nodding quietly.
her mother's hand swallowed her head.
there was whisper from the root
telling her to be still.
she died as she gave birth.
the child lived without ever hearing
or speaking.

she lived in the shadows of the house
and was taken care of all her life
sometimes coming out in the daylight
rocking back and forth
with a smile on her face.
her arms and legs folded to her body.
the sun deep inside her eyes
walking to the river.

Another Face

Small eyes water on the branch
they have been there
for a long time now
thinking:
please move your wings
to show me I have found you
at last.

***

this rock halfway out of the snow
turns away from the daylight
and cradles small blue footprints
into its stomach.
at night, they mark the snow again
keeping close to the rock.

Celebration

the little girl dressed
in purple,
a pattern of sealed eyes,
comes to the foot
of our bed,
signals her presence
and runs away from us,
dropping from her fingers,
a handkerchief filled
with well-chewed peyote,
fifteen cups of steaming tea,
wet circles in the wood
on the floor,
the name of the man who
chewed the peyote into
a ball.

outside, i see
through the frost
on the grass,
a snake,
coughing out hundreds
of babies in her dream
of falling,
dreaming of the young boy
who takes half of the green
roundness in his mouth,
hides the other half
on the bone of his wrist,
inhales the smoke from
burning sheaves of corn.

the snake is a woman,
her hair the sound
of horses,
an arm walking over
the soft white spots
of a frozen river.
she breaks through the ice
and two hearts float
to the surface.
each bearing her mouth
and my nose.

men with wings
of smoked birds,
porcupine heads,
dance under the sun,
under the lights
of mingling medicines.
the people in their dancing
pause to hear the laughing
of drunks, the other
drums along the ridges.

at home, away from
the celebration,
a girl tears herself open
with a clothes hanger,
smears herself on the windows
in loss of her half-brothers.

black dogs walk away
from the campfires.
the singers grow weary
under the shade of damp
branches, gather their heads

to the middle,
talk among themselves
about a trick song,
two deaths in one day,
and the girl whose
parents rushed home,
scraping their daughter
off the walls,
leaving her eyes
to the east.

In Missing

the stars in your face
reflect on the window
and glow right on through
to yesterday, floating
past the gathered boars.
the prints of my hand
on each boar collects
the winter as it appears
from the sky a few times.
i want to think the trees
are actually hearing
me think. it was an
accident and i'm sorry
for the trees stripped
of their bark, the shells
of humans and locusts.
the snow has come down
on my body and i sense
a face looking out from
my teeth. i tell the face
not to reveal me to the man
wrapped in a blanket with
rope.

my fingers are wrapped
in blue material, on
a white string, in knots,
like small bundles.
i am the wall of these
coughing sticks. i fly
down to a woman who believes
there are children packed

somewhere in her belly.
i ask her to convey to me
what is wrong and she sits
still for awhile before she
cries, bits of tobacco
and words fall from her
brown tongue. she looks
at her young sister,
points at her and turns
herself into a tree covered
with strings of colorful
beads that strangle the buds.
my head detatches itself
from me and i see my eyes water
as they go up the branches.
i feel the struggle of their
small arms, hear in their ears
a story of a man who took his
daughter's miscarriage into
the light of the kerosene lamp
before taking it into the night.
i feel lost. somewhere i remember
my grandmother pointing to
the ground over a bent tree
saying she had buried somebody
into the earth with her red
hands.

Coming Back Home

somewhere inside me,
there is a memory
of my grandfathers
catching robins
in the night
of early spring.
the snow continues
to gather children
outside, and i think,
as long as they are moving.
the frost sets itself
on the window before
the old man's eye.
we sit together
and imagine designs
which will eventually
vanish when the room
and talk become warm.
he goes over the people,
one by one, and stops
at one, because he can't
find any answers as to why
she took the sacred rattle
and used it, as if she were
one. they do not like her
much, he says. the same old
crowd will be out of
jail soon, and then,
back again. the trees
will be running with
sweet water and hard work
is to be expected.

so we covered everything
with quick conclusions
and sometimes there were
none, better to be left alone.
i pressed my fingers
against the window, leaving
five clear answers of the day
before it left, barking down the road.

Trains Made of Stone

until that sun, which keeps
asking for an answer,
agrees to remain still,
I will sleep without pain.
inside the sacred bone,
a final moment is breathing
and hard ways are mixed
deeper into long winters.
the choice has been here,
waiting for my decisions
whether i will turn old,
spinning hazily through
stories just once more
to feel like a keeper
of importance. i remember
roads being fed on sundays,
with my body that always
staggered home, touching
everyone with my life.
i would wake in dark fields
wondering if i had helped
the people who were like me.
it was then when sadness
leaned against my blankets,
making me sit up, secreting
yellow drops of light to make
my mother see. i knew of her
feelings as well as the past.
i believed in this walk
after death towards the west,
i was the slender bird within
this people of rainwater eyes

praying beside a well, near dawn.
these clouds drifting off
were my friends and the wind
in their favor continued
to speak of endless defeats.
the old woman held evil and
wanted to be known as the
foreteller of death.
my little sister danced as
a part of day, leading the others
slowly towards a time when all
things would be reversed.
i was away and news of her fight
carried inside me, telling me
that the river will never swell
behind our house and give birth
to lies. i have found life this
way and i will leave like one,
knowing that it has not passed.

Rushing

yellow november
comes swaying.
i feel the hooded man
drawing move on my cousin's
back.
black pellets drop
to the floor.
their ears full with
his lungs is the rush
of his bundled-up
life.

bits of bread,
pie and cake are placed
in a dish.
i smoke a cigarette
for him and bury
his clothes on
a hillside where once
a fox chased his face
away.

i feel no safety
as the shovel changes
into a shotgun.
i heard that in the night
a deer whistled out his name
from a cornfield and gave
him its antlers,
spreading his thoughts
through the dark.

years later,
as i warmed the shadow
inside my jacket over the stove,
my mother found a spring
and she brought the first
taste to everyone in a tin
silver cup, passing it
around,
drinking her words.

in some mornings,
as icy as it was,
i washed my face in it
sometimes thinking
of the hooded man and the fox,
the rushing sounds of a river
under our house.

The Crow-Children
Walk My Circles in the Snow

the buffalo breathed quietly inside
past visions of winter
as he thought of one time
when he stood on some far hill
with a shiny red blanket on his back
warmed by a bird who blew rain
into his eyes and saw
old white wolves lying on their thin bellies
gathered into a circle and eating the ground
that bled as if it had been torn
from an enemy's shoulder during battle
or a child's heart,
suddenly coughed up without reason
but the times then
were hard and too real to be accepted
like a grandmother asking you
to comb her hair in the daylight
and you know she wants to tell you
what she saw and felt:
there has been someone floating around here
last night
carrying a small bundled bag
pierced by long sharp bones.
it has waited long enough
grows afraid and wants to take another person.
again it has sent a green fire through
our small land
freezing ears and anything
within its glow stands still.

for only through this way
it can be sure of not stopping
on its travel somewhere
and seeing its shadow on the morning ground
with the sun ripping its face apart
and dividing the skin to the eager crows:
the crows crying like women
when they find themselves talking to each other
in their master's voice
their children throwing up small green pieces
of warm flesh
and looking confused when their throats
suddenly leap out at the thought of white wings.

The Cook

with the thinking of winter
no longer enclosing her
to her room,
the combing woman with the mirror
smiled as she watched the lard can
swing from the cook shed.
the kettle chains would soon
be unwrapped from the newspapers
and it refreshed her to know
she would soon be asked
to cook for praying families,
to laugh among the other women.

the image in the mirror
played with her.
it folded her face carefully
into the sides.
here was the other person:
the one who knew exactly
what she felt and thought.
the person in the mirror told her
it was there for a purpose
and that was to double her knowledge
of roots, hanging them on string
from wall to wall in her house,
arranging them by the power
of their use.

when it was time to bleed
the mirror knew first and it
showed her by fogging up the windows
of her house.

the birds with their breath
would then come, drawing pictures,
and feeding her clothes
to the fire.

she felt the birds were disappointed
in being what they were,
always walking up the trees
and counting holes endlessly,
shining the sun off their stomachs
onto her hands.
she would rub her hands over
her face and every time she did this
the rain would come out from the fields,
breaking the winter and spring
apart.

as the weather divided,
the birds watched the combing woman's
lips, reminding them of their own
shadows, three dwarves in search
of tobacco.

A Remembrance of a Color
Inside a Forest

a long ways.

i have approached
carefully.

ladies inside
the smoky room—

have quickly
frozen.

maybe a sidewalk
shares too
many secrets.

i no longer
see rivers.

each line—
each word—

seems to hold me.

a faith with
rainy eyes
has no differences.

i have no
other choice—

i am a part.

a soft day
overcomes me.

"i hope you
don't mind."

This House

i begin with the hills
lying outside the walls
of this house.
the snow and the houses
in the snow begin somewhere.
the dogs curled against each
other must feel they own
the houses, the people
in each house must feel
they own the dogs
but the snow is by itself
piling itself over everything.

i keep thinking of protection
such as a dog stretched over
a house with its guts pulled
out. its legs over each corner.
it is truly a dream to tie down
a skinned dog like a tent over
a house, watching it shift
as the wind changes direction,
like cylinders of pistols,
the holes of magnums turning
people inside out.

my young wife turns under
the yellow blanket in her sleep.
she wishes to be left alone,
closes herself within the dark
of her stomach, cups her hands
and sees what is ahead of us.
she senses i will die long before

the two of them, leaving her
without a house, without roomlight.

the yellow blanket, the house
and its people cover her.
the clothes she wears cover her.
the skin of her body covers her.
the bones cover her womb.
the dog feels it owns the womb,
protects the child,
encircles itself to a star
and dies in our place.

Black Dog

the black dog has again opened
its belly to the stars,
lifting the deer by their legs
and smiling at their hooves
cracked open by the winter.
like before, the dog's ears
quickly stand, sucking up
the disguise of leaves
from my skin, taking away
the steam of medicine that
had cleansed me of human scent.
the rocks inside the canvas hut
quietly cooled and the poles
from the river moistened
with the dew of plants.
the dog with its one eye,
turning blue in the sun,
attracted the crows and they
stood among each other,
holding council to see who
would be chosen to eat the eye.
while spearing for carp,
looking through the clear ice,
i saw deer hooves tumbling
along the river current,
scaring the fish, kicking
up the sand.
unsure of its meaning,
of what the hooves could represent,
i went home thinking that soon
i would miss myself as a father,
that i should not look at the sky

for fear the land would dry.
my back was to the east the day
they buried our son into the frozen
ground.
he is asleep inside the earth.
the water splashes on his face.
he fails to release himself
from me, his hands on my arm.
i dream of trading faces,
relieving his blood and memory,
pushing my hand deeper into the dog's
brilliant eye.

War Walking Near

death designs swirl high above faces that are
    of disbelief.
a captured people dressed in red hold hands and hum
to themselves a strange song.
brown rain slips fast into the old man
who visioned the coming revolution.

he tells to his reflection a small word
not to reveal that in the night
he controls the night enemy
night-enemy-who-takes-us-with-magic-medicine.
he heard the eagle with eyes of war walking near.
they say the spring air comes without much intention.

A Poem for Diane Wakoski

your blood does not flow, not even a little.
the spinning of fathers is useless—
you weave no patterns, not even a word.

the row of dead purple men squeezed
into your darkened brain. each one has
a memory of cigarette burns slowly
turning into gods upon your shoulder.
they merge from your ears and infect love.

Glossary

The following words used in this collection may be unfamiliar to some readers. The definitions, supplied by the poets, relate to the words as they are used in the context of the poems.

Ahunwogi—Cloth or skin wrappings worn as turbans (Cherokee)

An-na-du—Come (Chinook)

Asi—A small, earth-covered house used as a sweat lodge (Cherokee)

Camas—A blue lily with edible bulb which was a staple in the Salishan diet; from the Nootka word for sweet

Chee chako—Newcomers (Chinook)

Chuska—A mountain in northeastern Arizona

Elwah—A river in the Klallam home country

He-noh—The Thunder Spirit

Ho-had-hun—The Olympic Mountains (Nisqually)

Kachina—Ancestral spirits of the Hopi, personified in religious rituals by masked dancers

Kwatee—The Changer of Quinault mythology

Long Person—Literal translation of the Cherokee for river; in this case, the Oconuluftee River in South Carolina

Lukachukai—A Navajo community northwest of Ft. Defiance, Arizona; also a mountain range in northeastern Arizona

Maheo—The Great Spirit (Cheyenne)

Memp-ch-ton—Mount Olympus, Washington (Klallam)

Mox-pooh—To lie still and then explode (Chinook)

N'huia-wulsh—Village of White Firs, now Jamestown, Washington (Klallam)

O-le-man—Chief, strong one, or old man (Chinook)

Seatco—An evil spirit greatly feared by the Salishan people of the Washington and Oregon coasts

Sge'—Listen (Cherokee)

Swimmer—A-yu-ini, a Cherokee historian interviewed by James Mooney in 1888

Tamoanchan—Aztec paradise

Tchindii—A Navajo deity often represented as a coyote

Tlanusi' yi—The Leech Place; those areas of the Hiwassee River in North Carolina believed to be inhabited by giant leeches

Toe' osh—Coyote (Laguna)

Tsaoi-talee—Rock-tree boy, N. Scott Momaday's Indian name

Tsen-tainte—White horse

Uguku—Hoot owl (Cherokee)